© Ted Rose

SURE-FIRE WHITETAIL TACTICS

SURE-FIRE WHITETAIL TACTICS

The Ultimate Guide to Deer-Hunting Success

JOHN WEISS
FOREWORD BY PETER J. FIDUCCIA

Skyhorse Publishing

Skyhorse Publishing books may be purchased in bulk at special discounts for sales promotion, corporate gifts, fund-raising, or educational purposes. Special editions can also be created to specifications. For details, contact the Special Sales Department, Skyhorse Publishing, 307 West 36th Street, 11th Floor, New York, NY 10018 or info@skyhorsepublishing.com.

Skyhorse® and Skyhorse Publishing® are registered trademarks of Skyhorse Publishing, Inc.®, a Delaware corporation.

Visit our website at www.skyhorsepublishing.com.

10 9 8 7 6 5 4 3 2 1

Library of Congress Cataloging-in-Publication Data is available on file.

Cover design by Tom Lau
Cover photo credit: iStockphoto

All interior photos by John Weiss unless otherwise indicated.

Additional photos: p. 30—Florida Game & Fresh Water Fish Commission; p. 42—S.C. Wildlife & Marine Resources Department; p. 45—Ohio Division of Wildlife; p. 104—Maine Sport Fisheries & Wildlife by Al Goldman; p. 109—Virginia Commission of Game and Inland Fisheries by Kesteloo; p. 135—Ontario Ministry of Natural Resources; p. 137—Roman Jaskolski and p. 151—John Phillips. All illustrations by John Weiss unless otherwise indicated. Charts on pages 43 and 44 by Wayne Laroche.

Print ISBN: 978-1-5107-0815-0
Ebook ISBN: 978-1-5107-0816-7

Printed in the United States of America.

Table of Contents

Foreword

There are thousands of communications professionals within the outdoor industry, many of whom specialize in writing about white-tailed deer. Only a handful, however, have been able to achieve the level of respect and esteem from both their readers and peers as John Weiss has garnered. This is a testament to his skills and knowledge on all aspects of hunting whitetails.

Long before I became involved in an outdoor career, I regularly read magazine articles and books about deer-hunting strategies in publications such as *Field & Stream, Outdoor Life,* and *Sports Afield*. Interestingly, the deer-hunting articles in these publications that I consistently deemed as noteworthy and filled with concise information almost all seemed to be penned by John Weiss.

Weiss was among the few "chosen" whitetail pros that highly recognized top outdoor magazine editors, including Vince Sparano, Lamar Underwood, Jay Cassell, and Sid Evans, entrusted to supplement the pages of their magazines. It is no surprise that these editors favored him, as his highly informative data and expertise have the ability to take a reader's deer-hunting tactic skills to the next level.

Weiss's writing style has always been straightforward. He gets his points across to his readers without an excess of propaganda or elaboration. More importantly, his skills and understanding of the white-tailed deer's biology, behavior, and anatomy is impressive and second-to-none. In fact, of the countless whitetail authorities in the outdoor industry, Weiss's stock is like fine heavy cream—it naturally rises to the top.

Weiss's writings make it crystal clear that he has gained his deer-hunting skills the hard way—through trial and error and inevitable total success. As a highly competent deer hunter he evolved into a superb deer-hunting authority. For decades, Weiss's position as one of the nation's most prolific deer-hunting communicators has been unchallenged, and he continues to be a standout in the deer-hunting community.

No matter how many articles or books I have read by John Weiss there is always one constant. I enjoy reading and gain knowledge from his writings each and every time. That statement continues to hold true in a re-reading of Weiss's classic *Sure-Fire Whitetail Tactics*.

In this book, you will find countless tidbits of solid advice written in an easy-to-read and comprehensible manner. Weiss addresses many topics that hunters want to know more about including: whitetail staging areas, the effects of moon phase, how to locate and hunt funnels, the different stages of the rut, and how to use aerial photos. Here he shares his most guarded whitetail strategies in order to help readers put their tags on a mature white-tailed buck. Other chapters include cultivating food plots to attract deer, GPS secrets, and one of my favorite chapters—how to learn to stop a buck dead in his tracks from more than 100 yards away!

I can assure anyone reading this book that whether you are a seasoned veteran deer hunter or a novice, you will gain valuable deer-hunting skills and benefit from the know-how from the pages within this volume.

After you have finished reading this book, I'm certain you, too, will be impressed with Weiss's deer-hunting expertise and that he will become one of your favorite deer-hunting authorities.

—Peter Fiduccia, Award-winning journalist,
TV host, and author
Summer 2016

Chapter 1

Terrain Aerial Photos Tell All

Because the definition of scouting is "an attempt to find something by conducting a search," the deer hunter who does not make use of aerial photos cannot possibly hope to take home big bucks on a regular basis.

One exception to this rule is an acquaintance of mine by the name of Mule Morris, who lives in central Tennessee. Morris, then sixty-five, has taken a nice buck every year he has hunted. The reason for his success is that he hunts exclusively upon the 520-acre homestead farm where he was born and has lived all his life. As a result, if you know him well, and are able to gain permission to hunt his acreage, there's no need to do any scouting. Mule will simply point out any number of places where you can go sit on opening morning, and no matter which place you select, he'll bet a dollar your buck will be hanging in his barn by sundown. To the best of my knowledge, he's never had to reach for his wallet.

In virtually every other circumstance, however, aerial photos are essential to a hunter's success.

My regular hunting partner Al Wolter seconds that scouting axiom. For more than twenty years, Wolter worked for the U.S. Forest Service, managing hundreds of thousands of acres of national forest lands in several states.

"In fact," Wolter says, "the topographical maps we deer hunters have used for many years yield only a fraction of the information aerial photos do."

TAKING A CLOSER LOOK

A dedicated whitetail hunter with more than 100 bucks to his credit, Wolter religiously uses aerial photos every hunting season. He's puzzled as to why others do not utilize this invaluable tool as well.

"I can remember sitting in my office studying aerial photos to compile a new forest management plan for a given region," he recently recalled, "and it was often difficult to pay attention to my work. I began spotting generation-worn deer trails leading to and from food plots such as mast-bearing oak trees, and this tempted me to begin evaluating how animals were living and moving in that specific area. After that, I'd sometimes even begin daydreaming where I'd place a stand to have the best chance at bushwhacking a nice buck."

Aerial photographs came into widespread use in the early 1930s when Congress passed the Agricultural Adjustment Act. This was during the Depression, and the goal of the AAA was to assist farmers in establishing and maintaining a balance between crop and livestock production and national food-consumption needs. It quickly became apparent that virtually any landform could be measured and studied in only a fraction of the time with aerial photos than by actually walking the ground, dragging surveyor's chains, and then drawing maps.

Since then, three other agencies of the U.S. Department of Agriculture—the Farm Service Agency (FSA), U.S. Forest Service (USFS), and Soil Conservation Service (SCS)—have come to rely upon the precise visual information provided by aerial photos. Those photos are now used to assist in conservation practices, forest management, urban development, pollution studies, drainage programs, boundary determinations, watershed planning, road construction, and even tax assessment. The combined aerial photography files they maintain presently cover about 90 percent of the nation.

HOW TO OBTAIN AERIAL PHOTOS

USDA offices generally maintain photo files only for their specific county-by-county regions. In most instances, these photos are in 10x10-inch black and white format and in scales ranging from one inch = 4,833 feet to one inch = 200 feet. Digital film scans from any film available can be made up to 12.5 microns or 2136 dpi. Original film is used whenever possible

Aerial photos are designed to be viewed with a stereoscope.

providing a standard TIFF image from 0.25m to 1m resolution depending on original film scale.

If the particular photos you're interested in are not on file in the county seat where you plan to hunt, agency officials will help you fill out the necessary order form, which is then emailed to apfo.sales@slc.usda.gov. Your photos will arrive, rolled up and in a tube, in approximately three weeks.

It's important to note that although you can look at and study an aerial photo, just as you would a common photo that you might take yourself, an aerial photo is not like a one-dimensional topographic map. Far from it. Most aerial photos are taken with the intention of being viewed in stereo pairs with a handy little device known as a stereoscope (photo above). Compact models of stereoscopes intended for field use are available through stores that sell engineering supplies and surveying equipment.

A stereoscope gives you a three-dimensional look at the landscape, which is critical if you want to really learn about the terrain structure. In so doing, it's like watching a 3-D movie in which you can see deep into valleys and river bottoms while the higher elevations literally jump out into the forefield of view. There is simply no comparison between looking at an ordinary topo map comprised of an artist's contour lines and having an intimate, first-hand look at the environment as it really is through a stereoscopic examination of an aerial photo. Another advantage to using a stereoscope is that the device magnifies what you're looking at by 2.5 to five times what the naked eye would see in studying the same photo. This provides a wealth of insight because, just like fish, deer use terrain contours in their travels, and even ten-foot changes in elevation may have a pronounced influence upon their directional movements.

SCOUTING FROM YOUR LIVING ROOM

In my own pursuit of whitetails, I use aerial photos in two distinctly different ways, and both have vastly enhanced my understanding of the habitat I'll be hunting. This, in turn, has helped me better understand the behavior patterns of resident animals.

When I first start studying unfamiliar terrain, I look at photos in stereo pairs with a stereoscope (photo on page 5). This tells me more about the area in less than one hour than I could learn in several days of hiking around on foot. Scouting, then, need only be undertaken in a minimum amount of time, at a later date—and this only to confirm what I already basically know, plus to look for smaller, recent signs that obviously would not be present on the photos, such as rubbed saplings and scrapes.

Next, I bring into play a much larger aerial photo of the same tract of land. Mine is 24x24 inches and I have mounted it in a sturdy picture frame. The frame protects the photo from wear and tear but, more important, the glass front allows me to write on the photo with a grease pencil (see photo on page 6). This lets me mark the exact locations of physical sign that I discovered while scouting, property-line boundaries, where stands have been placed, or even logistics for staging drives. This is invaluable, especially when I'm hunting with friends who are unfamiliar with the region and need a visual reference as to where stands are located, what routes they should take

Small-format photos are supposed to be studied in pairs. This yields
an in-depth stereo effect that's similar to the view one would have in
flying over the landscape.

as drivers, or even how to negotiate the terrain when participating in cooperative still-hunts.

CONDUCTING THE SEARCH

Any tract of good deer-hunting habitat may reveal slight changes from one
season to the next. Consequently, the glass covering my aerial photo allows
me to erase last year's information and draw in the types and locations of
this year's crops, the whereabouts of any ponds which may have recently
been built, areas where logging may have been undertaken, perhaps where
a forest fire ravaged the landscape, and, of course, any new scrapes, rubs,
and other deer sign that I have discovered.

To provide an example of the wealth of insight that can be gleaned
from an aerial photo, consider the trees and how the following quick-
identification procedure can tell you what hunting tactics might be in
order even months before you actually set foot in the woods (photo on
page 6).

On aerial photos, large, mature trees always appear as big dots to the
naked eye, while immature trees appear as small dots; with a close-up look
through a stereoscope, you'll next be able to see the crowns and branches.

Obtain a large-format aerial photo and put it in a picture frame. This allows
you to write on the glass with a grease pencil to indicate recent scouting finds.

If those big dots are relatively light-colored, they are mature hardwoods that should be producing mast crops such as acorns, beechnuts,
hickory nuts, or the seed-fruits of maples or poplars, to name a few. This
tells you where a prime fall/winter food source is located—a source
that animals are sure to visit regularly. Yet, from your previous hunting experience, you also know that such mature trees create a high,
overhead canopy that prevents sunlight from bathing the ground; this,
in turn, means there shouldn't be much ground-level cover for midday
bedding purposes or for deer to hide in when hunting pressure begins
to intensify.

Conversely, if you see light-colored, small dots thickly saturating a
tract of real estate, those are immature hardwood saplings not yet bearing
annual mast crops. Deer may be able to browse here upon the occasional
buds and branchtips that are within their reach, but any prolonged activity
will probably consist of bedding in nearby regenerative brush cover. Major
feeding will occur elsewhere, so use your stereoscope to look for trails
entering and exiting this bedding area. The trails will appear on the photo
as thin, white, threadlike lines.

On aerial photos, dark-colored large dots indicate the presence of
mature conifer species. Since you know that spruces, pines, firs, and other
evergreen species constitute only starvation rations for deer when they
cannot find more desirable foods, and since such species likewise shade out

USDA   12   618080   579-21

With a panoramic look at the terrain, a hunter cuts his scouting
time in half. He can study ridges, clearings, and even deer trails and
potential bedding areas.

vegetative understory growth, you know in advance that these areas are
not likely to be used by deer for much of anything.

If those dark-colored dots are small, however, you know it's an immature conifer plantation; since such trees have dense whorls of branches close
to the ground, they provide ideal security cover for deer, either for bedding
or for hiding shortly after opening-day hunting action begins to heat up.

Moreover, if your aerial photo shows trees that appear as large, light-
colored dots, and if they are systematically laid out in evenly spaced rows
and tree-to-tree intervals, you know what that means. You've found an
orchard (photo above)! If the trees in question are bearing apples, peaches,
or plums, they'll be magnets for deer. Now scrutinize the perimeters of

the orchard for thick concentrations of small, dark-colored dots indicating bedding cover in the form of immature, dense pines, and the bulk of your scouting of that area may nearly be finished, right from the comfort of your living room! Later, all you have to do is hike to that specific edge where the security cover borders the orchard to ascertain exactly where to place your stand.

IN THE GAME

One year, while hunting in Alabama, we used an aerial photo to help us take three nice bucks in as many days. The photo revealed a ten-acre clearcut that wasn't visible from any of the back roads winding through the region. Beginning about three or four years after an area has been logged-off, regenerative growth affords deer with splendid browsing opportunities. Finding this particular clearcut would have been a stroke of luck or required extensive scouting on foot.

Aerial photos are so precise that even the species of individual trees and their ages can be identified. This old orchard was first found by studying a photo and then later double-checking it on foot for deer activity.

Yet once we were aware of the clearcut's existence and its exact dimensions—all of this having been ascertained while still at home in Ohio—we actually were able to pick out specific trees that would be likely candidates for portable stands, even though we had never actually visited the region!

After studying an aerial photo of your intended hunting grounds, it seems logical that finding and interpreting deer sign would mostly be a matter of visually seeing and examining it during scouting missions. That is true to some extent, but you also must be able to relate sign found in one area to sign found in another, in order to figure out how the animals are using the topography.

This brings us back to our earlier mention of the value of using a grease pencil to mark each and every find on your aerial photo; if you don't make use of an elaborate, framed photo with a glass front, at least paste your photo to a board and cover it with a clear plastic overlay. In this manner, various discoveries that may otherwise seem to be happenstance may suddenly, when viewed in conjunction with other located sign, begin to bear clear relevance, with a pattern emerging. For example, what you initially thought was an incidental scrape may actually be one of many in a rather straight line between a feeding and distant bedding area.

The bottom line is that through the use of aerial photos, you'll learn far more about your hunting grounds than you ever imagined possible. And when you know almost as much about the terrain as the deer themselves, your accumulated knowledge and insight will begin translating into a higher level of hunting success.

Chapter 2

Scouting and Track Analysis

For generations, books, magazine articles, and seminars by hunting experts have addressed various methods for patterning trophy bucks. Unfortunately, most have involved generalities instead of practical methods or specific details that an average hunter can put to use in the field.

Always consider the effect other hunters will have upon deer behavior. Roadside pull-offs where day hunters park and others camp will become hubs of activity that deer will retreat from.

One thing we're recognizing more each year is that big-buck success hinges not only upon outsmarting the animals themselves, but also on dealing with hunting pressure in a specific area. This greatly complicates the scouting process. Aerial photos used in conjunction with topo maps can be especially valuable for this. Here is the game-plan most experts adopt.

SCOUT THE DE-MILITARIZED ZONES

On a table, lay out the topo map of the area under consideration for this year's hunting. Next, use a highlighter (such as yellow or light blue) to color in all the terrain within 1,500 feet of either side of every road or trail a vehicle or four-wheeler can be driven upon; this is easily done by keeping in mind that on standard 7.5-minute series topo maps, three quarters of an inch equals 1,500 feet. You can eliminate this ground from any

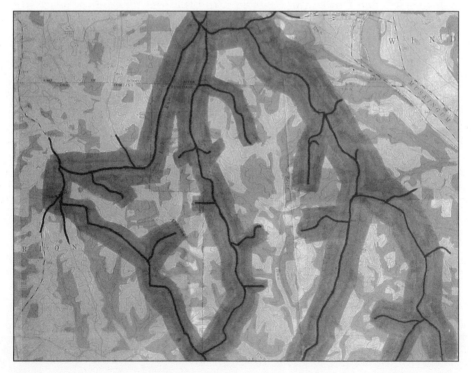

Since most hunters don't hike far from roads, use a topo map and a pen with see-through ink to indicate these areas of hunter influence. Scout beyond those zones of hunter activity and you'll find twice as many deer.

consideration because the chances of taking a nice buck there are between slim and none.

Studies of hunter pressure on deer have shown that most hunters do not venture farther than a quarter of a mile from some type of road or trail, and a quarter of a mile just happens to equal 1,500 feet on a topo map. Some of these hunters are simply lazy, but most of the others don't make use of maps because they probably fear becoming lost. As a result, these zones of hunter influence constitute hubs of human activity the deer won't tolerate for more than a day or so, especially during the firearms season.

If you therefore work somewhat farther back into the woods, you'll actually double your chances of seeing deer. Not only will you encounter the resident trophy deer that prefer such undisturbed habitat in the first place, but as the days pass you should also begin seeing immigrants that have retreated from the hunter influence zones bordering each road.

It is at this point that aerial photos should be brought into use to further narrow the search, as described in the previous chapter, whereupon actual scouting for sign can begin. Keep in mind that the techniques we've just described apply to public hunting areas only. On a large tract of private land, where only a select few have hunting permission, or in a sparsely populated region where hunting pressure is minimal, you may wish to rely exclusively upon aerial photos.

Once afield, tracks, droppings, and beds can yield a wealth of information, but only if they're interpreted properly.

NEW INSIGHTS ON TRACKS

In past decades, biologists attempted to solve the riddle of distinguishing between buck and doe tracks. Among them were Dr. Fredrick Weston in 1956, D. R. McCullough in 1965, and J. L. Roseberry in 1975. Their findings were largely futile and gave birth to the notion that the only way to be sure a set of tracks were made by a buck is to see the deer actually standing in the tracks!

Then along came Wayne Laroche, a research biologist from Vermont, who has turned the deer hunter's world upside-down.

"Like most hunters, I used to tell tales about big deer tracks and using rifle cartridges to gauge their size for as long as I can remember," Laroche recalled. "But this really isn't a very scientific—or accurate—way to home-in upon a big buck. Yet since it is common knowledge among biologists that dimensions of an animal's body typically increase as an animal increases in weight, I decided to find out if there is any relationship between the weight of whitetail bucks and their track dimensions that can be accurately measured in the field."

One of the startling things Wayne Laroche discovered is that the width of a track more accurately describes a buck's size than the length of the track does.

By artificially making tracks using hooves removed from deer carcasses, Laroche found that the natural shape of whitetail hooves causes the length of tracks from each hoof to vary considerably depending upon the hardness of the ground. Understandably, as ground hardness increases, less and less of the raised pad at the rear of the hoof is imprinted in the tracks. As a result, tracks on hard ground provide clear impressions of only the front part of the hoof.

Conversely, under soft ground conditions (mud, snow, loam, sand), the hoof sinks farther into the surface, with increasingly more of the raised rear pad of the hoof, and even the dewclaws, included in the print,

Hunters once believed the length of a deer track indicated the animal's sex and age. Biologists now tell us it's the hoof width, which slowly increases with age and body growth, that distinguish bucks and does.

thus making the track longer. "Dewclaw imprints in particular can greatly mislead hunters into thinking a given set of tracks were left by a buck," says naturalist Dr. Leonard Lee Rue III. "Since both bucks and does have dewclaws, the fact that they show in the tracks does not indicate the deer's sex. The only thing it indicates is that the ground was soft when the animal left the tracks."

Additionally, the toenails of deer grow and wear constantly, as do those of all hooved animals. This abrasive wear, to greater or lesser degrees, hinges upon the predominant nature of the animal's home range, which lends truth to the old adage that mountain bucks tend to have rounded hooves and swamp bucks tend to have sharp, pointed hooves.

All of this is precisely why the length of a deer track isn't reliable in evaluating the animal that made the track. The ground conditions under which a track are made may be so variable that a given buck may actually leave a large number of tracks of different lengths, depending upon the route he takes over and across different terrain conditions.

"It's an altogether different story with hoof width," Laroche explained. "Maximum hoof width occurs just in front of the rear margin of the hoof's toenail, near the middle of the hoof. Since the bottom of the toenail contacts the ground as a more or less flat surface, a deer leaves its maximum track width regardless of the degree of ground hardness."

While it's true that hoof width may vary slightly depending upon whether or not the animal has splayed its toes—as a deer does for increased stability when running across mud or other soft or slippery terrain— Laroche's field observations have revealed that the average toe spread of a deer walking normally is about one quarter inch. As we'll see later, it's important to keep this in mind when actually measuring tracks.

"Beginning in the fall of 1990, I took hundreds of measurements of white-tailed buck hooves with known, dressed weights ranging from ninety-seven to 244 pounds," Laroche described. "To make sure my data base was as accurate as possible, these measurements were made of bucks taken from the pre-rut, rut, and post-rut periods in order to reflect the differences in body weights that bucks experience throughout the fall/winter seasons of the year."

After performing a statistical evaluation known as "regression analysis" on the maximum hoof width and dressed weight data, Laroche found very strong relationships confirming that hoof width is a solid indicator of a buck's body weight. It naturally follows that bucks with the heaviest body weights are the most likely to be mature animals with the largest trophy racks.

"Now that I had developed equations that could be used to accurately estimate the weight of whitetailed bucks by measuring the width of their tracks, another problem arose," Laroche explained. "I knew it would be awkward for a hunter to make calculations or refer to tables while in the field. So I designed a lightweight plastic caliper that I named the 'Trackometer.' It's completely weatherproof and conveniently fits into one's pocket. When the caliper is adjusted to span the inside width of a particular deer track, it automatically indicates on a printed scale the body weight of the animal."

With a tool for measuring deer tracks, still another hurdle had to be contended with. Namely, how does a hunter looking at tracks distinguish between those from the front feet and rear feet?

This is important because still another of Laroche's stunning findings is that in the case of mature bucks, their front hooves are larger than their rear hooves!

"Since the front and rear hooves of mature bucks differ in maximum width, it's necessary to first be able to tell which is which before using the Trackometer to determine the animal's true body weight," Laroche said.

"Keep in mind that walking and slowly trotting whitetails place their rear hooves directly into the tracks of their front hooves. For this reason, all clear tracks left behind by unalarmed, slowly moving deer are tracks of the rear hoofs. On the other hand, running deer swing their rear legs ahead of the front tracks. Therefore, tracks made by both the front and rear hoofs are clearly visible."

BODY WEIGHTS ARE THE KEY

In going back to the subject of body weights being the most likely indicators of mature animals, it has long been documented that big-bodied does are extremely rare.

What this means is that if a hunter measures a deer track with a Trackometer and discovers that the body weight of the animal that left the track exceeds the 140-pound mark, there is a 98.8 percent chance the animal is a buck!

Moreover, according to the Vermont data, only one doe in 1,000 exceeds 160 pounds in weight. As a result, a measured deer track that indicates an animal exceeding 160 pounds means there is a 99.9 percent degree of certainty the animal is a buck!

Why don't does grow as heavy as bucks? Although genetics probably play a role, the most logical explanation is that lactating does expend a great deal of energy rearing fawns. An average whitetail doe begins bearing twins and heavily lactating at about three years of age, whereupon annual growth remains essentially flat. According to studies published by the Wildlife Management Institute, the body weight of a doe at three years of age is the approximate body weight she'll carry for the rest of her life, or until she becomes barren and ceases bearing offspring. Yet just the opposite is true with bucks. They continue to grow and steadily put on weight until they are at least seven or eight years old, whereupon tooth wear begins to limit food intake and the animals, and their racks, begin to degenerate.

This is invaluable insight. When using a Trackometer, and determining that a given track represents an animal exceeding 170 pounds in body weight, it is virtually guaranteed that not only is the animal a buck but that it is at least four and one-half years of age.

The reason this is so crucial to a hunter's scouting is because the magic figure of four and one-half years of age is the turning point in which a buck has grown from a teenager into a mature adult that is beginning to achieve the largest antlers he will grow in his lifetime. And, likely as not, he's the dominant buck inhabiting your hunting grounds.

Even more eye-opening, if the track-width measurement indicates a deer exceeding 190 pounds, the buck is probably at least five and one-half years of age and may be a potential candidate for the record book.

Of course, keep in mind that average whitetail body weights and track sizes may vary slightly around the country in accordance with the particular subspecies living in each locale; as a result, the very largest-bodied animals are far more likely to inhabit the northern Border States and Midwest than the Deep South. In time, however, a hunter who incorporates track-measuring strategies into his regular scouting routines can easily determine what constitutes tracks made by big bucks in his own region.

Although the Trackometer is a new and important tool that enables hunters to evaluate a buck's age and body weight by measuring its track width, it is by no means the only clue for distinguishing buck tracks from doe tracks.

Although it is probably impossible to tell the difference between tracks of mature does and small, immature bucks, most hunters who have spent

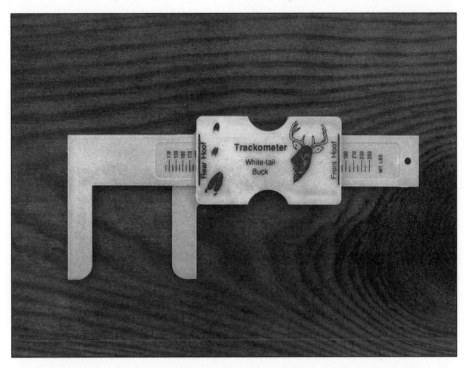

The Trackometer tool can tell a hunter to within 98 percent accuracy if a track was made by a mature buck.

any amount of time tracking whitetails will agree that the tracks of mature bucks reveal certain definable characteristics. Careful observation reveals daily activities that provide direct evidence of the many behavioral differences between the sexes.

Again according to naturalist Leonard Lee Rue, "big bucks, especially during the rut, tend to walk with a stiff-legged gait which causes an outward arcing of their feet. In other words, the tracks often appear to toe out. Conversely, small bucks and does tend to lift their feet higher and swing them forward in a straight line when walking, due to their relatively narrow body width and more even distribution of weight over the front and hind legs.

"As with the presence of dewclaw imprints lying to you, the presence of drag marks in snow supposedly indicating the track of a buck is yet another wives' tale," Rue continued. "Drag marks are made by bucks and does alike by the tips of the toes as they begin to straighten up so that their bearing surface is brought horizontal to the ground just before the next step is made. As the deer continues to walk, the front of the toes leave just a slight forward 'slice' in the snow as they leave the track to take the next step."

Another feature of walking tracks of big bucks is a distinctive staggered pattern that suggests a spraddle-legged gait caused by the increase in body width, which accompanies the increase in body mass of big bucks.

Laroche also notes that should the deer you are tracking urinate, more clues to sex will be visible. A doe's tracks will show that she has hunched back on her hind legs and urinated in her tracks, leaving a wide spray pattern. Bucks don't hunch back. They urinate straight down, leaving a narrow slot–like pattern that sometimes continues to drip as the buck moves on.

Studying deer sign is important to understanding their whereabouts and activities. Hunters with advanced knowledge can examine such sign and accurately predict the age and sex of the animal that left it.

Chapter 3

Deer Pellets and Beds

Deer droppings can tell a hunter a lot more than where a deer left the remains of last night's dinner. Recent biological studies have revealed that deer pellets can be analyzed by the casual hunter afield, allowing him to make a highly accurate guess as to the sex of the animal, how old it is, and even what the deer was eating.

An observant hunter can study deer droppings and accurately determine the age and sex of the animal that left them.

"The story of man's preoccupation with deer droppings in this century starts with the flashes of insight of Ernest Thompson Seton and his classic deer scatology illustrations," explains biologist Dr. Rob Wegner in his popular book *Deer & Deer Hunting* (Stackpole Books, 1984).

"By the late 1930s, deer researchers began to use droppings as an index to deer populations, thus going well beyond Seton's descriptions and illustrations. By the 1960s, scientists refined their survey method to the point where they could determine the species (plant composition) of the droppings by pH analysis. By the mid-1970s, they were baking the droppings at 60 degrees C in forced-air ovens and measuring their weights to determine the eating habits of their makers via microscopic identification. Today's statistical and computerized analysis of deer droppings, with their complex mathematical equations, simply overwhelm the mind of the deer hunter, if not the mind of the deer biologist as well. In central Utah, researchers now statistically analyze deer droppings with range-area data extracted from Landsat satellite imagery."

HOW MANY DEER?

Much of this new information has been filtering down to hunters in the know, enabling them to devise hunting strategies their fathers and grandfathers never dreamed of.

Examining individual piles of pellet droppings, for example, is a good way to gauge the size of a deer herd in a given area. After intensive field studies, biologists Creed, Haberland, Kohn, and McCaffery of the Wisconsin Department of Natural Resources have determined that whitetails defecate an average of thirteen times every twenty-four hours. With this insight, it's now possible for a hunting party to determine whether a prospective new hunting region is worth their time.

The most difficult aspect of this is recruiting the help of your hunting partners on a weekend to thoroughly scour one square mile of the real estate you might be interested in hunting come fall; studying only one square mile is sufficient, even though the actual size of the tract of land may be considerably larger.

On the first day, line up as if you were beginning a deer drive, but with your "drivers" much closer together than usual. Then, systematically hike the length or breadth of the terrain back and forth as many times as is necessary to cover the entire 640 acres; with five hunters participating, this should take the better part of the day. Additionally, each "hunter" should be armed with a can of biodegradable, yellow spray paint.

Each time one of you discovers a pile of deer pellets, give the pile a quick spray of paint, regardless of how old or fresh the droppings seem to be. Naturally, performing this type of deer census is much easier and far more accurate if done in February or March when there is either a very light skiff of snow on the ground or an absence of vegetation; this makes spotting the pellets easy from a distance, as compared to summertime scouting when plant life will obscure many pellet piles from view.

Your party of hunters should hike the same terrain the very next day. This time, each participant should carry a can of red spray paint, a notepad, and a pencil. Each unmarked pile of droppings discovered on this second day will be less than twenty-four hours old and will be easily distinguished from those droppings with the yellow paint, which are more than twenty-four hours old. The purpose of the red paint is to identify the fresh droppings so that they are not inadvertently counted a second time when you later sweep back through the same general area from the opposite direction. Each hunter should also record the number of new piles of droppings he discovers.

Finally, at day's end, total up the number of new piles of fresh droppings discovered by the entire party and divide that figure by thirteen to determine the number of deer present.

According to the Wisconsin DNR, a region possessing five deer or less per square mile should probably be discounted from consideration because it is unlikely that more than one of those deer would be a mature buck. In this case, it would be wise to scout another location at least several miles away, hoping for a pellet count to reveal at least fifteen to twenty-five deer per square mile.

Keep in mind that the Law of Diminishing Returns eventually kicks in with deer population densities; too many deer (more than thirty-five per square mile) is just as indicative of poor trophy buck production as too few deer.

In going back to the above example, if you and your partners counted a total of 247 fresh piles of droppings, that means there are approximately nineteen deer using that 640-acre tract of land you've just scouted, a clear indication you could expect reasonably good hunting in that region.

Admittedly, doing weekend pellet counts like this takes time and effort. But many hunting parties I know combine this activity with searching for shed antlers, which provides yet more valuable information pertaining to bucks that survived the hunting season and still are in the vicinity.

TAKING A CLOSER LOOK

"The type of food eaten determines the shape and consistency of deer excrement," says Dr. Leonard Lee Rue III. "This is valuable to hunters because it can furnish a clue to where deer have been browsing or grazing. If a deer has been feeding upon grasses, forbs, or fruit, its feces is usually in the form of a loose mass of very soft pellets. When the deer has been browsing upon drier material such as woody twigs and dead leaves, the feces will be in the form of elongated pellets that are quite hard."

"In the spring and summer," Wegner adds, "fresh pellets acquire a greenish or bronze hue, they tend to glisten, and they're very soft inside. Yet later in the fall and winter months, pellet coloration may range from shades of brown to dark mahogany or almost black."

But don't allow the effects of weather to fool you into thinking that pellets are fresher than they really are. Obviously, pellets will dry quicker in direct sunlight, in windy weather, or in low humidity than in shade, on still days, or in high humidity.

Moreover, old, dry pellets may appear shiny and fresh if subjected to rain, fog, or early morning dew. To determine whether this is the case, simply crush several droppings. Deer pellets always dry from the outside in. Therefore, pellets that glisten on the outside but crumble when squeezed are at least several days old. Conversely, pellets that shine on the outside but have the consistency of modeling clay inside may be only hours old.

PELLET SIZES TELL ALL

Perhaps of greatest value to hunters who learn how to analyze deer excrement is the possibility of determining the approximate age of the animal in question and whether the pellets were left by a buck or doe.

All of this boils down to the simple fact that, within a given species, older and more mature animals leave larger-size calling cards than young, immature animals. Also, within the same age category of animals of the same species, males always give off larger-size excrement than females simply because of their larger body sizes and larger internal anatomy.

Therefore, during the course of pellet-count surveys or any other scouting mission, an important tool hunters should make use of is a simple tape measure and notebook. Then, when pellet piles are discovered, record the average size of the individual pellets comprising those piles.

Keep in mind there are thirty different whitetail subspecies across the continent, and they vary greatly in body size and therefore the sizes of pellets they drop. In the region I hunt most often (the upper Midwest), the whitetail species is *Odocoileus virginianus borealis*, also known as the northern woodland deer, which is the largest whitetail subspecies.

My hunting buddies and I have learned that droppings which are one-half inch or less in length indicate a doe, yearling, or fawn; droppings that are five-eighths inch in length indicate a buck approaching maturity, probably a two-and-one-half-year-old; while droppings that are three-quarters to one and one-quarter inches in length indicate a trophy buck that's three and one-half years or older.

Conversely, in South Carolina, where *O.v. virginianus* resides, which also is known as the Virginia deer, average body sizes are considerably smaller; as a result, pellet sizes of all age groups and sexes will likewise be smaller. In other words, while pellets measuring one and one-quarter inches in length indicate trophy bucks in Ohio, Illinois, and Wisconsin, pellets measuring only three-quarters of an inch in the Palmetto State may very well represent the presence of mature bucks.

BUCK OR DOE?

Aside from pellet sizes, an even more intriguing way of determining whether a deer's calling card is from a buck or doe is presently under investigation.

Some researchers believe that, in most instances, doe excrement piles are in the form of individual, loose pellets ranging in number from twenty-five to sometimes more than fifty. They are also of the opinion that buck droppings are not only individually larger but are evacuated in greater quantity. Maryland deer biologist C. J. Winand's studies have concluded, for example, that bucks can be ascertained by dropping piles in which there are seventy-five or more pellets. Additionally, buck droppings are often clumped together in amorphous, walnut-sized or larger globs. This is especially the case when the animal's diet consists largely of succulent vegetation. Yet when killing frosts cause whitetails to make a transition from grazing to browsing, buck excrement becomes somewhat less mucous and

Biologists have learned that a deer defecates thirteen times a day. A mature buck's pellet pile contains an average of seventy-five droppings that average one and one-quarter inches in length.

adhesive and may be found in smaller, looser clumps that sometimes break apart from the impact of hitting the ground.

An area of speculation currently being debated by biologists is that although a deer's diet largely influences the shape, color, and consistency of its feces, another factor may be involved to explain the "clumping" tendency of buck droppings. Nutritional studies conducted by biologist Charles Ruth of Clemson University with penned deer during the non-rutting period have shown that bucks have a higher body metabolism than does, due to their need to achieve body weight more quickly. This suggests that previously ingested food passes through a buck's intestinal tract more quickly, causing it to become consolidated and compacted.

In referring back to the situation in which we described hypothetically finding 247 piles of pellets indicating the presence of nineteen deer, it's now clear that adding pellet-size information and pellet-clumping charac-teristics of bucks to the picture can broaden your insight immensely. An astute hunting party may actually come to the conclusion, again hypotheti-cally, that of those nineteen resident animals, fourteen are does, yearlings or fawns; four are mature two-and-one-half-year-old bucks; and one is three and one-half years or older and must undoubtedly have a very impressive rack.

As a result, while many hunters often become preoccupied with find-ing big tracks, large scrapes, and rubbed saplings, the most encouraging scouting reports are those in which members of our party describe finding clumped droppings with individual pellets averaging one inch or longer.

THE BEDDING CONNECTION

Conducting a diligent search for droppings during the course of scouting missions can, in still another way, greatly assist in piecing together the puz-zling lives of deer in a given region. While whitetails may defecate almost anytime or anywhere, which explains the occasional finding of droppings on a trail or in a meadow where they have been feeding, the most pellets are found in an altogether different location.

According to Dr. Wegner's research, there is irrefutable evidence that most whitetails defecate shortly after rising from their beds. Moreover, the quantity of pellets around the periphery of the bed indicates the length of time that a deer remained in that particular spot.

This is important insight when it comes to deciding upon a strate-gic stand location. Perennial advice given to deer hunters is to situate a stand somewhere between the deer's feeding and bedding areas in order to ambush them as they go back and forth. Well, ascertaining feeding areas is not difficult, especially in farm country, but finding bedding areas can be an exercise in frustration.

The reason is because whitetails—especially bucks—rarely bed in the same spot each day. Rather, they have general bedding "areas" and, there-fore, each bedding episode seldom leaves a well-pronounced, matted oval to be easily detected by the hunter's searching eyes. The two exceptions to this are the presence of snow or damp leaves.

Always take the time to evaluate beds found under such conditions. Beds measuring forty inches or less in length indicate a doe, yearling or fawn. Beds forty-five inches in length indicate two and one-half-year-old bucks, while beds that are fifty to fifty-six inches in length indicate three and one-half-to six and one-half-year-old bucks. (Again, these figures will have to be adjusted slightly downward in regions where specific, small-bodied whitetail subspecies exist). Furthermore, look at how the beds relate to each other. Two or three small beds accompanied by one large bed usually represent a doe with her current offspring. A lone bed, especially if it's located on higher ground, is nearly always that of a mature buck.

In the absence of visible beds in snow or damp leaves, many individual piles of both old and fresh pellets in a relatively small area saturated with dense cover is a sure indication of a bedding area. Closer examination of the pellets should next offer clues to the ages and sexes of the animals and, following this, it should not be difficult to determine the most probable route the animals are using when they travel to nearby feeding areas.

When scouting, take a small tape measure. Beds you find that are fifty to fifty-six inches in length are those of mature bucks.

Finding concentrated numbers of droppings, which reveal bedding areas, is important in two other ways. Within the home range of each whitetail is an approximate forty-acre "core area" where the animal spends up to ninety percent of its time. This core area offers the best combination of desirable attributes to be found within the animal's much larger home range. There will be easy access to water and a prime food source, to be sure, but of even greater concern to deer, and especially mature bucks, is that the core area will be virtually free of human disturbance. In short, a core area offers a buck a greater sense of security than anywhere else within his home range.

Consequently, when hunting pressure begins to mount and the biggest bucks in a given region become almost exclusively nocturnal in their

Studies with radio-collared deer have shown they rarely bed in the same exact spot every day. Rather, they have general bedding areas in high-security regions seldom penetrated by humans.

feeding, drinking, and other activities, you know exactly where they'll be sequestered during the daylight hours. They'll be hunkered down in their beds, somewhere in their core areas. Because you've already determined the location of those bedding regions by finding and analyzing their droppings, staging an effective drive or cooperative still-hunt with a partner should give you a good chance for success.

If you prefer to hunt solo, keep in mind that bedded whitetails always lay with their legs splayed to the left, facing downwind; in this manner, the animal can scent-monitor anything that might attempt to approach from directly behind him where he cannot see, and he can see very well in the other directions in which he cannot smell.

The fact that deer always lay on their right side, facing downwind, is important to keep in mind. If the wind is from the south, for example, a careful stalk from the east, advancing toward the bedded deer's blind side, would be more likely to succeed than a stalk from the north, west, or south.

By the same token, even when hunting pressure is light or nonexistent, these safe bedding areas are the places to check when storm fronts move through the region, assaulting the landscape with severe weather and causing deer to seek seclusion.

Chapter 4

Antler Rubs: Communication Signposts

I came upon the huge rub while hunting squirrels, not while scouting for deer. And an unusual discovery it was, because this was in early September, a full six weeks before Ohio's bowhunting season opened and more than two months before the rut. Moreover, I'd never seen a pine tree so ravaged. It was entirely stripped of all its bark to a height of about five feet off the ground, and its former branches had been reduced to an array of sorry looking, broken stubs.

This happened twenty years ago, and I was destined to hunt many additional years before I'd look back and appreciate the significance of that particular rub. I'm also confident that I know the very buck that made it. The animal undoubtedly was the huge 12-pointer old man Harley Wilkes killed on this, his farm property, and it was the biggest deer he'd seen there since his father homesteaded the place during the Great Depression.

Two decades later, I was an avid student of noted whitetail biologists Larry Marchington, John Ozoga, James Kroll, and other university luminaries, all of whom earned PhDs in large part from engaging in research projects dealing with antler rubs and the complex method of communication among both male and female deer.

We still do not fully understand every aspect pertaining to rubbing behavior, and even among the most respected scientists there is occasional disagreement on certain fine points. Nevertheless, every year new information surfaces. The astute hunter who keeps abreast of these findings is sure to refine his knowledge of whitetails, and it is this very educational process which translates directly into more and bigger bucks hanging on the meatpole.

But first, let's dispel a few long-held wives' tales. To begin with, antler rubs do not indicate places where bucks have removed their velvet and then polished and sharpened their tines.

When a whitetail's maximum annual antler growth has been attained, the skin-like velvet dies, dries, and begins falling away in shreds, mostly of its own accord; the entire shedding process is often completed in less than eight hours. About the only time a buck hastens its removal is when an annoying, stringy remnant hangs down and impairs his vision, whereupon he briefly thrashes his antlers on a nearby shrub.

Scientists tell us bucks do not rub trees to remove their antler velvet. The velvet naturally dries and peels away, and the underlying tines are already smooth and sharp at their tips.

Once the underlying antlers are fully exposed, the main beams are already smooth, and the tine tips are pointed. There is no need for the buck to hone them like a gladiator readying his swords for battle.

The height of the rub is also not of any importance, which is yet another myth that supposedly indicates the size of the buck that made it. After all, deer sometimes stand on their hind legs when making a rub, and it is not unusual for a very limber sapling to bend all the way over, enabling even a young buck to straddle the trunk and rake it all the way to its uppermost crown of branches.

On the other hand, the diameter of the rubbed tree is indeed significant, with the largest diameter trees indicating large bucks and smaller diameter trees representing the work of younger males. But here again, you must be careful in your analysis of rubbed trees and not simply restrict your search to large rubs. The rule of thumb is that big bucks sometimes rub small trees as well as large trees, yet it is very rare for small bucks to rub large trees.

The occurrence of a big buck rubbing both large and small trees is undoubtedly a combination of happenstance and planning. As we'll discuss in a moment, the deer wants to leave numerous calling cards, in the form of olfactory signposts, to alert as many does as possible to his presence, so he rubs all manner of trees. But he will also specifically target a number of

Antler rubs are signposts bucks use to communicate visual and olfactory information to other deer. The diameter of the tree rubbed indicates the buck's approximate age.

unusually large diameter trees to rub, to create visual signposts, in order to warn other mature males that this is his breeding territory.

As to the exact significance of individual antler rubs, most biologists believe they serve the purpose of enabling each buck to establish a breeding territory of sorts. It should be emphasized that whitetails are not territorial in the true sense of the word, as it would be quite impossible for even a dominant buck to drive all other male deer out of his several-square-mile home range. As a result, in most regions, several or perhaps many bucks must share the same turf.

Still, despite the fact that whitetails are not territorial, they must nevertheless acquire a breeding area where they feel secure, while simultaneously obtaining a social status that gives them breeding privileges over subordinate or lower-ranked animals.

TIMING THE RUB

There are two distinct periods when most antler rubs are created. The first rubbing activity usually occurs during the first three weeks of September, when bucks are still in their bachelor groupings. Now is when they are developing their herd rankings. This is when they decide, within their local society, which are the superior "alpha" deer and which are the subordinate "beta" deer. Moreover, the very first rubs are made by the dominant bucks in the region, due to their anxiety to get on with the business of firmly establishing the herd pecking order. How many rubs does a mature buck make? According to deer biologist Marchington, who has studied the subject intensively, a mature buck makes anywhere from sixty-nine to 538 rubs in any given year, with each buck making an overall average of 300 rubs! With the peak rubbing period of mature males being the first three weeks in September, this means a dominant buck can be expected to make at least fourteen rubs per day.

Insightful hunters should therefore mark on their aerial photos or topo maps the exact locations of the first rubs they discover during early scouting missions, as they were likely made by the largest deer in the immediate area. Confirmation of this suspicion, of course, comes in the form of noting the sizes of the rubs; they should be at least two and one-half inches or larger in diameter.

The second flurry of rubbing activity takes place during the first week of October. This is when the other, lesser deer in the region instinctively engage in their rubbing.

THE MAST CONNECTION

Another revealing thing we've learned about whitetails is that a buck's antler-rubbing behavior is directly tied to seasonal mast production. When there is a bountiful mast crop, a hunter can expect to find a much higher number of rubs than usual. Conversely, in years when mast production is low, rub densities may be thirty to sixty percent less than that of the previous year.

The reason is that a buck's physical health is dependent upon mast. Acorns, in particular, but other types of mast as well, are transition foods that deer utilize shortly after hard frosts kill the lush vegetation they've been feeding upon during spring and summer but before they've fully switched to browsing upon twigs and branch tips. As a result, when there is a poor or virtually non-existent mast crop, the mid-fall physical condition of the animals deteriorates just enough to reduce the vigor and intensity with which they engage in pre-rut rubbing.

Keep this in mind when you are scouting, and if you are not finding as many rubs as you'd expect, don't automatically conclude there aren't many bucks around. Take the time to check a number of oak ridges or hardwood forests to evaluate the mast crop. If you find little mast, bucks are most likely in the area, but they are simply rubbing less that year. On the other hand, if mast is plentiful, but rubs seem markedly absent, chances are the buck population is indeed quite low.

TIMING THE RUT

Interestingly enough, biologists now have reason to believe that the peak of the rut may change slightly from year to year as a result of bucks having the ability to influence the estrus cycles of does.

Essentially, what happens is this. When there is a greater number of buck rubs in a given area than normal, it's quite likely that an earlier than usual estrus will take place among local does because of so-called "priming pheromones" deposited on trees by bucks. These scents, when deposited in greater quantity than usual, have been found to induce early ovulation in does, pushing the peak of the rut forward.

For example, in one Michigan study, the average peak rutting date in an area with only a marginal number of bucks was determined to be November 11. Yet five years later, when there were more and older bucks in the same area, the peak of the rut had advanced to October 23.

Therefore, while hunters in past years commonly asked their local wildlife officials when the peak of the rut occurred in their state, and then intensely hunted during that time, such a practice is no longer recommended, since the advice may be off by as much as two weeks in either direction.

Instead, hunters can now more accurately determine when local rutting activity is destined to occur by diligently scouting for rubs.

In my home state of Ohio, for example, I had long accepted the Division of Wildlife's proclamation that the peak of the rut is November 15. But I now know this is only a statistical average of the past twenty-five years, and that the coming deer season may see frenzied rutting activity as early as November 1. This was exactly what happened during the 1994 deer season, and I knew about it in advance, because as soon as autumn leaves began to fall, innumerable antler rubs appeared almost overnight. Conversely, during Ohio's 1998 deer season, we found only a random rub here and there—far fewer than any other year I could remember—and, as we expected, this delayed rutting activity. In fact, we were seeing bucks chasing does as late in the year as December 10.

The priming pheromones deposited on rubs by alpha bucks not only induce early ovulation in does, but also have the effect of suppressing the already lower testosterone levels in young bucks. This well-ordered plan causes a region's subordinate bucks to not begin engaging in rubbing behavior until October and November, and thereby effectively reduces their aggressiveness and competition for breeding privileges.

In nature's mysterious way, this well-planned scheme is designed to benefit the herd. Young bucks, which are chemically induced into a low position in the breeding hierarchy, engage in minimum reproductive effort and therefore experience less late-season weight loss. They are thus better able to make it through the upcoming harsh winter months and are more likely to grow to larger and healthier sizes the following year, when they are destined to become dominant breeding animals themselves.

PINNING DOWN YOUR BUCK

When a buck leaves his bedding area, heading in the direction of a known food source or making his rounds to check scrapes, he occasionally rubs saplings adjacent to the trail he's traveling. In time, distinct rub lines are created. Savvy hunters can interpret these signs and, with a high level of accuracy, ascertain the direction the animal was traveling and even the time of day the buck made the rub. With this information at hand, being in the right place at the right time come hunting season becomes much easier.

But first, one must have a general idea where to begin conducting his search for rubbed trees. Again according to biologist Marchington and his research, 26 percent of all rubs are found along deer trails, 10 percent along old logging trails, and 15 percent along stream banks in valleys. The remaining 49 percent are random rubs created along field edges, woodlot clearings, in the vicinity of thickets, and throughout forested regions.

Because of this, it makes a lot of sense to investigate such locations, especially where there are pockets of terrain known to have aromatic trees such as cedars, pines, spruces, shining sumac, cherry, and dogwood. However, according to biologists at the University of Georgia, a whitetail buck's No. 1 choice of species to rub upon is the sassafras. Despite the fact that sassafras comprises an extremely small percentage of trees in most forests east of the Mississippi, more than eighty percent of the largest rubs discovered in study areas were found on sassafras.

In the absence of these species, bucks will create rubs on virtually any species, but they distinctly like the ones listed above. The most commonly accepted explanation for this preference is that the oily, resinous cambiums of these species will retain the buck's forehead gland scent longer. In the case of non-aromatic species, much of the scent deposited during rubbing activity is likely to wash off during the next rainstorm, thereby making the rub less effective as an olfactory signpost.

TAKING A CLOSER LOOK

As mentioned earlier, hunters should take a topo map or aerial photo of their hunting area, and mark the locations of each rub they find, especially the season's first rubs, which are indicative of the largest bucks in the region. If this isn't done, each discovery may seem totally happenstance. But when you can study large numbers of individual rubs on a map, your perspective broadens, and a pattern can often be discerned that reveals distinct rub lines and thereby the trails a buck is using.

With this accomplished, it's time for a closer investigation of the individual rubs comprising the overall rub line.

If the tree is rubbed on the downhill side, you can bet that it was made in the morning when the buck was ascending to his midday bedding area; hence, you've found a trail worth watching during the morning hours. Conversely, if the rub is on the uphill side of the tree, the deer was invariably coming downhill in the evening to feed or search for ready does in the lower elevations; this trail calls for an evening stand.

A similar situation takes place in flat terrain, with rubs found in open feeding areas and around the perimeters of woodlots generally having been made during the night hours and rubs deep in heavy cover generally having been made during midday.

During the course of his scouting, a hunter may chance upon an area of intense rubbing activity where it seems like virtually every tree within fifty square yards has been ravaged. Upon seeing this, the hunter's first thought is usually that a monster buck's pent-up anxiety and sexual frustration caused him to go berserk.

To be sure, anything is possible in the world of whitetails, but according to biologists, what the hunter most probably found was a rub concentration that is not overly significant, at least in terms of pegging the whereabouts of a mature buck.

Rub concentrations are created early in the season when bucks are still in their bachelor groups. If there are two or three bucks keeping company, and they are all of the same age-class and carrying antlers of roughly equivalent size, chances are they're having difficulty sorting out their hierarchal rankings and determining who's who on the totem pole. This is especially true among immature one-and-one-half or two-and-one-half-year-old bucks.

As a means of intimidation, one of the bucks is likely to rub a sapling while the other two watch. Another buck is then likely to respond by saying, in effect, "oh yeah, well watch this!" whereupon he demonstrates his prowess by rubbing another tree. The third buck then predictably responds by putting on his own show. This rubbing activity can go on for an hour or more, and when the animals finally depart, it looks as though not a single tree has been left untouched.

Although the appearance of a rub concentration can be quite impressive, even awesome, it probably will not prove to be a good hunting location when the season opens. By then the bachelor groups will have long since disseminated, abandoned their late-summer/early-fall travel patterns, and adopted their own individual breeding territories elsewhere.

GETTING IT ALL TOGETHER

One of the best times to study whitetail rubbing behavior is early spring, before lush vegetation has had a chance to emerge and hide last year's deer sign. The exposed cambiums of rubbed trees will not have weathered yet, and trails will be easily discernible. Moreover, like the game "connect the dots," an astute hunter can often spot consecutive rubs leading off into the distance, and by drawing imaginary lines between them, he can determine that particular buck's precise travel pattern.

The value of this scouting exercise has many facets, just one of which is the possibility of finding shed antlers. That way, you know for sure that the buck who made the rubs survived the hunting season and approximately what his new rack will look like next year.

Additionally, keep in mind that mature bucks frequently rub the same trees from one year to the next. If you closely examine a fresh rub, you'll probably detect weathered scarring that has healed over from the previous season. Be absolutely sure to note the locations of these particular trees, because if the buck that created them survived this hunting season, he's almost sure to rub them again next year.

By following a rub line and its associated trail, a hunter can also ascertain the bedding area the buck is using. This is vitally important, as the hunter will not want to situate his stand too close to the bedding area.

Aside from the rubs of alpha bucks serving as olfactory signposts and thereby having an influence upon the estrus cycles of local does, their secondary and equally important function is to serve as visual signposts among local bucks. In effect, an antler rub is an extension of a given animal in that deer's absence, and it serves to communicate information to other bucks which may filter through that region at a later time.

Advanced hunters can use this insight in a very novel way, if they'll keep in mind that no matter where they're hunting, there's a likelihood that at least several bucks are sharing the same area and are even using the same trails.

When a buck comes ambling down a trail littered with rubs, an observant hunter should instantly know whether the deer is just a so-so deer or the dominant buck in the immediate region. If it's a subordinate deer, the visual stimuli of the large diameter rubs along the trail will cause him to outwardly display his inferiority. The most common submissive body posture exhibited by a low-ranking deer is a slinking gait that reminds me of a dog that has just been swatted on the rump with a newspaper for wetting the floor. The tail is held tightly against the hindquarters, the back is somewhat sunken, and the head is held low.

If a buck exhibits this behavior, you can take him or not, depending upon what fulfills your expectations for concluding a successful hunt. But realize that the deer is using body language that reveals, in no uncertain terms, that he is intimidated by the rubs in the area; and this means the trail in question is also being used by a much larger animal.

A dominant buck, however, is sure to reveal an entirely different personality. He'll proudly hold his head high and may actually have a somewhat prancing appearance to his gait, almost like a high-stepping quarterhorse. But the sure tip-off is that he will periodically lift his tail to half-mast and extend it straight back for long moments at a time. If you observe this behavior, you might as well go ahead and take the deer at the first opportunity, because, in that particular region, he's at the top of the social hierarchy. The only other alternative, if he is not what you're hoping to take, is to pull your stand and devote your remaining hunting time elsewhere.

In any event, the long and short of it is to find the early rubs. They're the best way to hedge your bet that you'll collect the biggest buck in the region you're hunting.

When hunting a rub-line, observe the behavior of any bucks that come along. This is a nice buck, but he's exhibiting inferior body posture, which tells the hunter it was another bigger buck that made this rub.

Chapter 5

Moon Phases and Latitude: The Rut Triggers

Hunters living north of the Mason-Dixon Line have become so conditioned to believe the peak of the rut is November 15 that quite often they actually miss the best rut-hunting action in their region.

Undoubtedly this goes back more than forty years to a widely published study conducted by New York deer biologists Lawrence Jackson and William Hesselton, who spent seven years studying the embryos of 864 road-killed does. By determining the ages of the embryos and then back-dating, it was possible to determine the date each doe was bred. The findings of the biologists concluded that a majority of the does were bred during a ten-day "window" spanning the dates of November 10 to 20; or, on the average, November 15, which is the date that has long since been stenciled on the foreheads of deer hunters.

It all sounds logical and scientific, but we've since become aware of flaws in the interpretation of Jackson and Hesselton's study; keep in mind, their work was conducted from 1961 to 1968. In the years since this landmark research, other scientists have made other investigations and learned that the onset of the rut may be triggered two weeks before or two weeks after November 15.

Now, after three decades of pursuing deer, I finally realize why some years I experience little or no rut-hunting action while other years the intensity of the rut can only be described as incendiary.

During those years when it seemed as if there was no rut, hunters could expect to see a plethora of magazine hunting articles offering various explanations. I always found humor in the articles that claimed that not much breeding took place, probably because of unusual weather that turned the deer off; proof that this assertion was false always came the following spring when a new crop of fawns could be seen following their mothers. Other deer-hunting writers, including myself, speculated that perhaps weather had indeed influenced the rut, and it was excessive heat or other adverse conditions that had simply caused the majority of the breeding activity to take place after dark.

Now, however, new research information has come to light that strongly suggests that, due to cosmic influences, hunters simply missed the rut because it occurred much earlier or later than they expected.

The rut is triggered by a combination of circumstances. The most important are the the region's latitude, the length of daily sunlight, and the moon phase.

WHAT TRIGGERS THE RUT?

According to Vermont biologist Wayne Laroche, there are five factors that can cause variations in the dates that deer breeding activity takes place from one year to the next.

The age structure of the local population has a critical influence upon the timing. Since young does breed later than mature does, areas that have high populations of young deer often have an almost unnoticeable first rut followed weeks later by a second rut that is quite intense. Conversely, if the local deer population has a high percentage of mature does, intense breeding will take place earlier than the norm.

The sex ratio of the local population is a determining factor because areas that have low buck populations have lengthy rutting periods of low intensity, simply because there are not enough males to impregnate all available females. Conversely, areas with high buck populations have shorter, more intense mating seasons in which the majority of the females may be bred in just a few days; in this latter case, if you've miscalculated and missed getting afield at precisely the right time, you're out of luck.

The health of the local deer herd is vital to successful breeding. Bucks and does that live on prime range and are in excellent body condition breed earlier and with more intensity than deer living on poor range.

The genetics of the subspecies inhabiting a given region are important because widespread transplanting of deer took place fifty to seventy-five years ago. For example, this is why Georgia whitetails, which were transplanted from Wisconsin, breed almost two months earlier than native whitetails living in neighboring Alabama.

Variations in latitude, as one travels farther north, cause the breeding season to be compacted and intense, yet as one travels farther south the rut is protracted and less intense. At the equator, there is no specific breeding period at all. Mating is subtle and takes place throughout the entire twelve months of the year.

DAY LENGTH AND LIGHT INTENSITY

"Trying to sort through all of this and get your ducks in a row is a real headache for the hunter," Laroche says, grinning, "but it's a real turn-on for research biologists.

"The earth wobbles in a cycle on its axis as it orbits the sun," Laroche continues, "and it's this solar cycle that sets the breeding season for whitetails in non-equatorial regions."

Interestingly, since fall in the southern hemisphere occurs at the same time as spring in the northern hemisphere, some peculiar experiments have been performed. In one study, northern US whitetails that always rutted in November were transplanted to New Zealand; they immediately shifted to an April rutting period.

The importance of this experiment is that it conclusively proved that whitetail mating behavior is not triggered and synchronized by calendar dates, but by annual changes in solar and lunar influences.

Whitetails have a pineal gland, sometimes called "the third eye," that is present in the brain of all animals having a cranium, including humans.

Some years it seems to hunters that no breeding activity is taking place. This is because the weather or moon phase triggered the rut to begin earlier than usual or is delaying its onset.

The sole function of this gland is the secretion of the hormone melatonin. How much of this substance is secreted is controlled by light intensity; low light levels stimulate the production of melatonin and high light levels inhibit it.

So how does an organ inside the brain know how much light intensity is taking place outside the skull? Researchers contend this information is received through nerve pathways from the pineal gland to the eye. Moreover, when light levels are low over prolonged periods of time, high levels of melatonin trigger the release of sex hormones from the pituitary gland to steadily bring the animal to a height of sexual readiness.

In northern whitetails, this date is approximately November 1. Look upon the scenario as a gun that first has been loaded and then cocked. It's ready to go off at the slightest impetus; in the case of bucks, it's the full moon that serves as the trigger. This is the pre-rut chase phase, when bucks do goofy things and act like reckless teenagers with their testosterone faucets wide open.

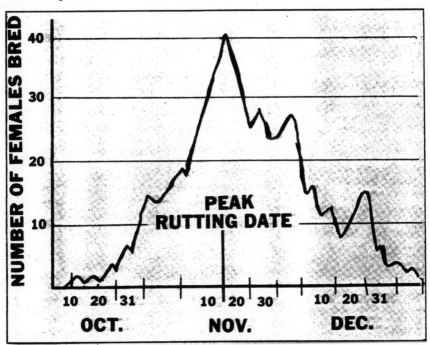

North of the Mason-Dixon Line, the average peak of the rut is a ten-day window in early to mid-November.

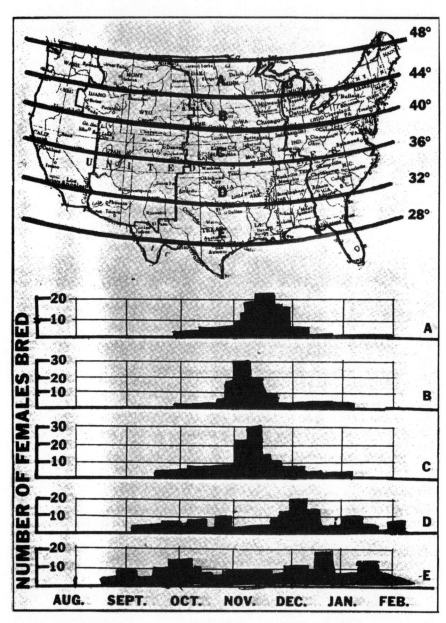

South of the Mason-Dixon Line, whitetail breeding activity becomes protracted, spanning many months.

The surge in the mating receptiveness of does occurs shortly thereafter, when the full moon ends and the so-called peak of the rut begins.

Why all of this is important to the hunter was the question that caused Laroche to develop a computer program demonstrating how deer rutting behavior changes in relation to diminishing light levels from day to day and week to week; equally significant, Laroche learned how rutting activity within the timeframe decreed by nature is slightly different from one year to the next.

What resulted was the Whitetail Rut-Predictor, in the form of a series of annual fall/winter calendars. At a glance, any hunter can scan the calendar of the current month and see that each day of the week has a representative symbol. These symbols tell him exactly what deer are doing on each particular day as solar and lunar influences steadily change and cause a subsequent reactive change in deer behavior.

The five calendar symbols are represented by silhouettes of bucks engaging in feeding, seeking, chasing, tending, and resting body postures,

Of the three-part rutting season, the pre-rut and peak rut are the most exciting because bucks are making scrapes, chasing does, and are responsive to calling and antler rattling. During the post-rut, bucks are exhausted and spend most of their time bedded.

each of which tell the hunter which hunting strategies are likely to be the most successful on each given day.

"If there is a seven-day stretch on the calendar depicting feeding deer, naturally you'll want to hunt each day at a prime food source," Laroche explains. "Little rutting action is evident as yet."

If several days on the calendar reveal bucks in a seeking mode, the pre-rut is underway and scrape hunting is now the hot tactic, along with using a grunt call and rattling antlers.

If there is a string of daily chasing symbols, the pre-rut is intensifying. Now, hunting doe-bedding areas and doe-feeding areas is undoubtedly the best bet, with a doe bleat call coming in handy. For the time being, the effectiveness of scrape hunting is beginning to taper off.

If tending symbols predominate, the peak of the rut is taking place. Now, calling bucks is futile. Hunting scrapes is getting even worse. Hunt doe travel corridors and use a doe bleat call or fawn bleater.

If there are a long string of resting symbols, the peak of the rut is over and exhausted bucks are trying to regain body strength. Since bucks may now lay up in their beds for days at a time without moving, stand hunting is a waste. The tactic of the day should focus upon gathering hunting partners and staging drives through heavy-cover bedding areas.

WHAT'S A "CENTRUS" RUT?

A similar method of predicting deer activity levels is the popular Moon Guide developed by Minnesota researcher Jeff Murray. Yet it's different from the standpoint that it doesn't focus upon the rut alone and therefore can be used throughout the hunting season.

"I've pegged three universal strategies in accordance with the moon's position, not its phase," Murray explains. "Confirmed by radio-telemetry studies, we now know that the best hunting success near open food sources is only when the moon is overhead near sunset, because during the rest of the lunar month deer won't show up until after dark. When the moon times occur during early morning and late afternoon, hunt bottlenecks or travel corridors connecting evening bedding and feeding areas with daytime feeding and bedding areas. And for the rest of the lunar month, hunt strictly near bedding areas.

"Regarding the rut, a three-year lunar cycle is comprised of early, middle, and late phases," Murray continues. "This is why hunters frequently

The Moon Guide is invaluable to hunters because it gives
the exact dates each year of a centrus (normal) rut, so
hunters will not miss out on the action.

claim to experience hot rutting action one year but little or no rutting the
next year. Actually, what happened was that they entirely missed the rut
because the deer's sexual cues were triggered earlier or later than usual.
Whenever the rut is on time, right in the middle of the lunar cycle, the
phenomenon is called a 'centrus rut.'"

I've found both Wayne Laroche's Whitetail Rut-Predictor and Jeff
Murray's Moon Guide to be highly accurate in assessing deer activities
across the northern half of their range. But since Laroche's research is based
upon a computer model of solar and lunar changes in various light levels,
and since Murray's is based upon moon position cues, localized weather

conditions may slightly affect those light levels and thus slightly accelerate or retard certain phases of the rut.

"For example," Laroche explains, "dense cloud cover shortens day length by fifteen to twenty minutes and diminishes the intensity of moonlight at the ground surface. Similarly, heavy rain or snow falling through the atmosphere blocks sun and moonlight by defracting and diffusing light, and this prevents nearly all moonlight from reaching the earth. Storm conditions may shorten day length by more than thirty to forty minutes each day. Conversely, a long stretch of bright, sunny weather tends to suppress deer movement and may delay the onset of rutting activities in other regions. As a result, weather-induced changes in day length may explain slight differences in breeding times at different locations each year at the same latitude.

This is why it's important for any hunter to stay in tune with what's going on in his own turf. Continuously dark, overcast weather in his region may accelerate all aspects of the rut by a day or more. Yet at the same time, his friend living at the same latitude 100 miles away, where the weather has been continuously sunny, may not see the onset of rutting activity for several more days or until dark clouds associated with a storm front move into his area.

Every year we continue to learn more about whitetail rutting behavior, but biologists admit that many mysteries still remain to be unraveled.

Chapter 6

The New Scrape Savvy

Few things in the deer hunter's world trigger adrenaline-pumping excitement like finding a fresh scrape with large tracks in it and then detecting the unmistakable, pungent aroma of tarsal scent wafting about the area.

So it wasn't at all surprising when one day I chanced upon a mother lode of scrapes that caused my hair to stand on end. In an area no larger than about two acres I counted eleven of the mating invitations, indicating a mature buck that had literally gone loco with breeding frenzy.

This electrifying discovery brought still another revelation. For the first time in a long career of pursuing whitetails, at this moment I no longer pondered whether the many mating invitations before my eyes were primary scrapes, secondary scrapes, boundary scrapes, or whatever. It just didn't make any difference what label a human might attach to them. In terms of whitetail communication, they all stood for the same thing . . . a very special place where a buck intended to repeatedly pass on his gene pool. Moreover, it was a place that literally screamed, "hunt here!"

Just two hours later I was back at the kitchen table in my southern Ohio farmhouse drinking coffee, having concluded the shortest deer hunt I've experienced in more than twenty-five years of pursuing whitetails; it also resulted in one of the largest bucks I've ever taken, an 8-pointer that field-dressed at 230 pounds.

ALL SCRAPES ARE NOT THE SAME

Unquestionably, all serious hunters look upon the peak of the rut as the highlight of the season, no matter what date it occurs in a particular region. And no wonder, because deer-hunting authorities have long said the only chink in a trophy buck's armor is that brief period of time when his hormones are racing out of control, compelling him to return to his scrapes time and again in the hopes of seducing estrus does.

"Some trophy bucks are so well educated and wary they are simply unkillable," Ohio biologist Tom Townsend recently said. "The exception is the peak of the rut, when they are inclined to do some goofy things. That's about the only time you might catch one of them being a little careless."

Scrapes, of course, are the catalysts that serve to unite male and female deer. And because biologists have ascertained that whitetails make at least six different types of scrapes—each with its own significance and level of importance in the social order to which deer rigidly adhere—understanding which specific scrapes should be eliminated from consideration and which others should be diligently hunted can go a long way toward helping a hunter consistently hang up nice bucks.

It can be extremely difficult to take a mature buck through most of the hunting season. One exception is the rut, when they're preoccupied with breeding and let their guard down.

ESTRUS-RESPONSE SCRAPES

An estrus-response scrape is the least likely to produce a buck sighting. When a doe approaches the onset of heat, chemical changes in her endocrine system are discharged whenever she urinates. If a buck happens to randomly chance upon one of these scent deposits, he'll instinctively make a scrape right there on top of the urine-dampened earth.

Estrus-response scrapes are easily identified for what they are because they seldom exceed eight inches in diameter and they are never found in association with a mutilated, overhanging tree branch. Most are found around the perimeters of fields and meadows where deer have been feeding at night, or in doe bedding regions, but they can be found almost anywhere else as well. If you periodically check back, you'll find these scrapes are not enlarged or freshened.

Of course, there is always a slight probability that you might take a buck in the vicinity of an estrus-response scrape. It should be emphasized, however, that a hunter's success in such an instance is usually the result of watching a general travel corridor that is occasionally used by deer. Otherwise, the scrape itself is merely a happenstance.

BOUNDARY SCRAPES

Boundary scrapes are a bit more complicated to describe, and they may or may not be productively hunted, depending upon several circumstances.

By description, boundary scrapes reveal all the usual signs of authenticity, except one. They are of average size, they are located beneath tree branches that have been broken and chewed upon, but they seldom seem as fresh and steaming hot as other scrapes one might find. The reason for this is because boundary scrapes are laid down around the outermost perimeter of a buck's home range, and they are therefore visited less frequently than scrapes located in areas where the buck spends most of his time.

Because boundary scrapes randomly dot the periphery of the buck's territory, knowing how to recognize typical home-range boundaries of deer will in turn help you to identify such scrapes. Although it sometimes seems as though whitetail bucks are inclined to go anywhere they damn well please, radio-tracking studies have shown that they actually spend as much as ninety percent of their time in an approximate forty-acre core area, in which they have the region's best combination of food, water, and security cover at their disposal. Furthermore, when they do periodi-cally leave the safety of their core areas to venture into surrounding or outlying regions, they are reluctant to cross major man-made or natural barriers (assuming, of course, that they are not being chased by dogs or

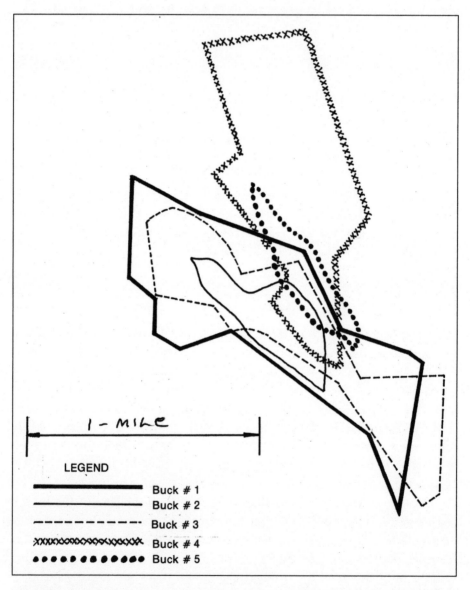

This radio-tracking chart shows the home ranges of five radio-collared bucks. Note how their ranges overlap and they share common grounds. Natural barriers often determine the boundaries of these home ranges.

being subjected to intense hunting pressure). Because these obstacles tend to restrict the bucks' travels, the obstacles, in large part, serve to establish the irregularly shaped home ranges (usually no more than two square miles in size) in which most bucks live out their entire lives.

Just a few examples of home-range boundaries, or barriers, include superhighways (especially if they are bordered by high fences), wide river courses, lakeshores, sheer rock bluffs, steep mountain ridges, canyon rims, and forest edges that yield to wide expanses of open prairie ground or human developments. There is a great likelihood that scrapes found along any of these types of well-defined edges are boundary scrapes.

Deciding whether or not to hunt boundary scrapes hinges upon first assessing the local doe population. If there is a high doe-to-buck ratio, I wouldn't hunt boundary scrapes; a buck has all the female companionship he can handle within the inner sanctuary of his home range, and there's simply no need for him to go looking elsewhere.

Conversely, if doe numbers are low, boundary scrapes may produce regular buck sightings. Bucks now need to travel far and wide in order to service the available does, and this means regularly patrolling not only their core area but also the perimeter areas of their home range.

DOE SCRAPES

A third type of whitetail scrape that is not worth hunting, and one that we've only recently begun to learn about, is the doe scrape. Yes, does make scrapes!

Interestingly enough, though bucks typically make scrapes by pawing the ground alternately with their two front hooves, does use their rear hooves. If you've ever observed the peculiar behavior of a dog as it vigorously claws grass and sod in a backward direction with its rear paws—most often, shortly after it has defecated— you can understand how does create scrapes in almost exactly the same manner. On only a few occasions, when observing penned deer at wildlife experiment stations, have I seen does make scrapes with their front hooves.

To date, we don't know why does make scrapes. Likely as not, these scrapes have some type of communicative significance in the social order of local deer. In any event, the only value in being able to identify these

Boundary scrapes sometimes are laid down around the perimeter of a buck's home range. They're important to know of only when a region's doe population is low and bucks must travel widely to find the females.

scrapes is that the hunter knows that a doe was standing in the scrape location at one time, and so possibly he can discern a trail that other does might also be using from time to time; when these females come into estrus, bucks engage in what's known as "trail transference," abandoning their own trails and temporarily monitoring doe trails instead.

There are several ways to distinguish between a doe scrape and a buck scrape. First, a doe scrape will seem crudely and superficially scratched away. As an analogy, imagine taking a garden rake and dragging it only two or three times through a small spot in the grass in your front lawn. Such doe scrapes just aren't nicely cleaned away to bare mineral soil or manicured around their perimeters, as are buck scrapes. In many instances, they are not even round in shape. Sometimes, such a scrape will have a long tube-like or oval shape because the doe scratched a few times with her hoofs, walked forward a step, and then scratched again. Finally, with regard to any type of doe scrape, you will not find the scrape in conjunction with an overhanging tree branch.

SECONDARY SCRAPES

At this point, it is important to say that all buck scrapes except one (the estrus-response scrape) begin life as secondary scrapes. It is not until many weeks later that a small percentage of these secondaries become elevated in status to either primary or community scrapes. Therefore, early in the season—up until early November in the northern states and up until about mid-December in the southern states—all scrape hunting will be done in the vicinity of secondary scrapes. There simply are no primaries in evidence at this time.

All scrapes begin as secondaries, and the majority are made on level ground. This buck is rub-urinating and will paw the scent into the ground to create the scrape. Mature bucks make an average of twenty to thirty-five scrapes per year.

As a rule, whitetails create scrapes in areas that offer a mix of mature and immature trees and successive understory brush and vegetation. They tend to scrape infrequently in large, endless tracts of mature forestland. And they rarely make scrapes on steeply sloping terrain. Try to recall the scrapes you've found in the past and I'll bet the majority of them—even those in mountainous terrain—were on level ground; in this case, the "flat" terrain may have consisted of nothing more than a narrow, terraced, hillside bench, but it probably was relatively level nonetheless.

Regardless of whether the overall real estate is flat, rolling, or hilly, biologists at the University of Georgia have determined that any given mature buck of two and one-half years of age or older will make an average of twenty to thirty-five scrapes throughout his home range. I've already noted that some of these will be outlying boundary scrapes that don't experience much re-visitation except in cases of a few does in the vicinity. Consequently, the secondary scrapes you'll want to begin hunting early in the season will be those located within the buck's core area.

Ascertaining buck core areas is a relatively easy matter that simply involves wearing down a good deal of boot leather. What a hunter particularly wants to search for is an abundance of concentrated sign in the form of tracks, beds, droppings, rubbed saplings, and scrapes. And especially in regard to tracks, beds, and droppings, the hunter should hope to find some sign that is very old, some that is moderately old, and some that is very fresh, as this combination is the best indicator of almost continuous presence of the buck in his core area over long periods of time.

In reconnoitering the terrain and deciding where to build a blind or install a portable tree stand overlooking secondary scrapes, I would caution against hunting too close to the bedding area. To a buck, his bedding area is the single most important place within his core area because it's where he feels safest during daylight hours. If you get too close and your repeated intrusions are blatant, the buck may lose confidence in his security cover and abandon the bedding area entirely.

If I could set the stage for hunting secondary scrapes early in the season, here are the circumstances I'd want to sketch into the picture. I'd be in a buck's core area, and I'd be in a tree stand at least 200 yards from the buck's bedding area. Moreover, that tree stand would be on the downwind side off one of the many trails filtering to and from the bedding area and upon which at least one secondary scrape is to be found. With this setup, I could quietly slip into my stand and then simply wait for the buck to make an appearance as he returns to his bedding site in the early morning or as he leaves his bedding site in the late afternoon.

It should be emphasized that hunting secondary scrapes early in the season is basically a hit-or-miss proposition in that all of the scrapes in the core area are of relatively equal value. In other words, the buck in question does not specifically favor one scrape over another, and his re-visitation is random. About the only way for the hunter to tip the odds slightly in his favor is by hunting those particular scrapes located on heavily-used travel corridors leading from bedding areas to feeding grounds. Or, hunt what are known as "scrape concentrates." These are places where you find numerous scrapes in a relatively small or confined area, such as the example I offered at the beginning of this chapter.

PRIMARY SCRAPES

A small percentage of secondary scrapes eventually transform into primary scrapes and begin getting each buck's special consideration and attention. Yet few hunters realize that it's the local does that elevate the status of these scrapes, not the resident bucks! How all this happens involves an intriguing bit of animal science.

In time, a small number of secondary scrapes will be elevated in status to primary scrapes that are frequently revisited and freshened. When this happens, ignore the other secondary scrapes and hunt only the primaries.

First, understand that whitetail bucks are not at all territorial; many bucks commonly share the same home range and, in many cases, even have overlapping core areas. As a result, the many secondary scrapes littering the woodlands in a several-square-mile region may be the products of perhaps a dozen bucks or more. These scrapes serve to inform the local does that these bucks are around, but more important, the does can smell the scrapes and determine the current state of health of the individual males in residence.

That's right: it is each doe that decides which particular buck she wants to breed with. A doe instinctively knows that the successful propagation of her species depends upon her successful impregnation by a virile, healthy male, and nature has given her a way to determine this. In smelling a buck's urine in one of his secondary scrapes, a doe is able to recognize certain chemical byproducts. Virile, healthy, mature bucks metabolize fats and carbohydrates, and they urinate the byproducts of this in much greater concentrations than do equally healthy but immature bucks. Furthermore, bucks that are old, beginning to degenerate in health, and are beyond their reproductive peaks, metabolize proteins, and this is equally evident in their urine.

In effect, then, each doe may investigate a number of scrapes made by different bucks before deciding which buck she wants for her sire and where she will allow the mating to take place. She then urinates in that appropriate scrape, depositing her own unique glandular secretions, and then she remains in the general area, waiting for the buck to return.

Upon making his rounds and randomly checking his secondary scrapes, the buck will suddenly come upon the doe-scented scrape, recognize it for what it is, and elevate this scrape immediately to primary scrape status. The buck then proceeds to scent-trail the doe until he eventually catches up with her, establishes a "tending bond" until the precise moment that she gives the "go" signal, and copulation is then usually completed in short order.

This apparently well-ordered plan, however, quickly turns into pandemonium as the rutting period intensifies toward its peak. This is because not every doe experiences her estrus cycle at precisely the same time. Furthermore, in any given region, there may be upward of fifty or more males and females, all healthy and capable of reproducing. As a result, a buck may finish the matter of impregnating one doe only to immediately thereafter take up the trail of another and then still another as he tirelessly checks and rechecks his various primary scrapes.

Correctly identifying primary scrapes is not difficult because they seem to be in a perpetual "muddied" state as they are repeatedly cleaned of windblown debris and freshened with new urine deposits. Conversely, the recently abandoned secondary scrapes will quickly become hard and dried out and partially covered with falling leaves and other forest duff.

From this point on, areas around primary scrapes are the places to hunt, at least until the rutting period is over and the deer return to their former activities.

Incidentally, too many hunters make the mistake of placing their stands too close to scrapes, and this invites their ready detection by returning bucks. As it often happens, a mature buck instinctively knows it's not necessary to freshen his scrape every time he returns to its general vicinity, so he'll often merely scent-check it from up to fifty yards downwind. To avoid detection, it makes sense to place your stand even farther downwind so the returning buck passes between you and the scrape, and with his attention focused in the direction of the scrape.

COMMUNITY SCRAPES

Still another type of scrape created by whitetails is perhaps the most fascinating of all. It is known as a community scrape and it consists of a primary scrape that is simultaneously used by several bucks that share overlapping core areas within their home ranges. Generally, the bucks in question are of the same age, have nearly equivalent racks, and therefore all rank about the same in the local pecking order. Because there is no rigid social hierarchy distinguishing the animals, a given scrape does not become the personal property of one buck or another, and it therefore is visited by different bucks, each hoping to eventually discover a doe's estrus urine. While there, the buck will clean the scrape, hook at the overhead branch with his antlers, and leave his own scent.

Consequently, if a hunter stays well attuned to the scraping activity in the region he's hunting, various members of his hunting party may all take nice bucks over the very same scrape over a period of several days. The initial requirement is that someone must first take a buck near a scrape. Then, someone must return to that very location to examine the scrape each day. If it isn't freshened within two or three days, it can be presumed the scrape was a former boundary scrape, secondary scrape, or primary scrape made by the animal now hanging on the camp meatpole.

Community scrapes are those visited by several bucks, usually in core areas where their home ranges overlap. Often, two or three hunting partners can each take a buck over just one of these scrapes.

However, if there are indications the scrape has been visited and freshened, you know for sure it's a community scrape. Get another hunter on that stand, pronto! There's an excellent chance he'll soon have a shot at another buck that's still using the scrape.

DOES PIPE THE TUNE

It was mentioned earlier that it's the does that select their mates, not vice-versa, and that they do so by chemically analyzing each scrape's scent.

In a way, does even determine, by default, where a buck will lay down most of his secondary scrapes. It stands to reason that any buck that's eager to breed wants his mating invitations to receive as much exposure to the local does as possible. So he predictably creates most of his secondary scrapes in the vicinity of where does spend a majority of their time . . . their core bedding areas.

On countless occasions I've discovered scrape-concentrates and then, upon closer investigation, found a doe bedding area nearby. The lesson is

It's the presence of does that determines where bucks will lay down their scrapes and which ones will be revisited. Never forget the axiom, "find the does and you'll find the bucks."

that whenever I'm unsuccessful in finding scrape areas, I try to recall where I've found doe beds in the past, and invariably I'll find scrapes nearby.

If it's a new area you've not scouted or hunted before, simply begin looking for the type of terrain does favor for bedding. Typically, they prefer to bed in thickets midway up a gentle slope, as opposed to bottomlands or along ridge crests. And they prefer sun-drenched, east-and south-facing terrain. The beds themselves can easily be identified by the matted ovals of varying sizes that are indented in the grass and leaf litter, and by large and small tracks leading in and out of the area. (The smaller tracks are those of the doe's current offspring and her daughter from the previous year, which will stay with their mother until her estrus cycle begins cranking up and she drives them off.)

Finally, it's essential to note that although finding a major rutting area is a virtual guarantee of deer-hunting excitement, this strategy has a limited

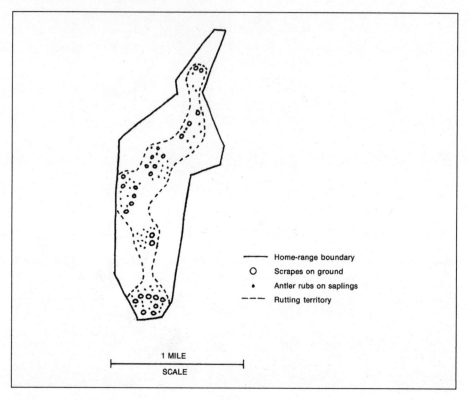

Home-range boundary
Scrapes on ground
Antler rubs on saplings
Rutting territory

1 MILE

SCALE

This radio-telemetry chart shows one buck's home range and the scrapes he laid down one year. Note the areas of concentrated scraping activity.

shelf life. Major scrape areas are at their productive best early in the season during the several-week pre-rutting period as a buck is in the process of advertising his services. The rut itself doesn't begin until the does come into estrus, and from that time on bucks spend less and less time revisiting their scrapes and more and more time traveling in the company of does that are allowing themselves to be bred.

Chapter 7

The Importance of the Second Rut

Every deer hunter can recall particularly memorable experiences afield. The one that forever changed my approach to whitetail hunting occurred just behind my country farmhouse in southern Ohio.

It was the week before Christmas, long after the conclusion of the whitetail rutting period, which hereabouts spans a time frame of about three weeks, from October 30 to November 20. Several hunters in our group had taken nice whitetails, but I was not among the lucky few. Now, with the wind howling and driving snow assaulting the countryside, I was engaged in one of my final chores of the year, hauling a pickup load of split firewood from one of our oak forests to eventually be stacked next to our kitchen door.

As I drove along, I glanced across a ravine and there, on a brushy hillside maybe 200 yards away, were two bucks with their antlers meshed, each trying to push the other back upon his haunches. They were really going at it, exhibiting all the pent-up sexual rage that mature bucks are capable of. Standing nearby was a doe, who nonchalantly watched as the two gladiators repeatedly butted heads and jockeyed for position in an attempt to gain an advantage.

I was beside myself with disbelief. The rut had supposedly been over for many weeks and yet here I was on the scene of what might well have been an early November mating frenzy at its peak. Eventually, one of the bucks conceded defeat, clamped his tail between his legs and bounded away through a thornapple thicket. The doe departed in the opposite direction, with the second buck hot on her heels.

BIOLOGISTS TELL ALL

That incident occurred just a few years ago, and it changed my pre-conceived notions about the annual whitetail rut. This also was about the time when several leading university biologists began intensely studying the subject and releasing new findings.

One of the most interesting discoveries of late is that white-tailed bucks do not really go into rut as many hunters continue to believe. Rather, it's the does that have very well-defined periods of receptivity, and the bucks simply accommodate them.

This was proven by an experiment in which a doe and a buck were placed in a large, fenced enclosure. During the course of the year-long study, the buck generally paid little attention to the doe. In fact, as a rule, he preferred to keep to himself. At various times, however, the doe was injected with a hormonal stimulant to artificially induce a state of false-estrus, whereupon the buck was instantly all over her. It did not matter whether the month was March, June, or December; once his nostrils were filled with the heady aroma of a doe in heat, he would not leave her alone!

Bucks don't really go into rut, as most hunters believe. There's a time span of six months when they're fully capable of breeding. So technically it's the does, which have a brief twenty-four-hour estrus period, that go into rut.

It should be noted that although a whitetail buck will attempt to mount an estrus female every month of the year, he's only capable of impregnating her when he has hardened, velvet-free antlers. It is only during this time frame—a period spanning the months of September through February—that his elevated testosterone level produces a high sperm count.

Nevertheless, the point is that it's only the does who experience very brief periods of sexual readiness. Therefore, from a technical, scientific standpoint, it's actually the does that go into rut, not the bucks.

Across the whitetail's range, hunters anxiously look forward to the so-called peak of the rut, as this is when deer mating activity intensifies to its highest level of the year. This is when bucks are so wired that they frequently throw caution to the winds. Yet the phenomenon is not the result of bucks suddenly experiencing a hormonal rush. Rather, it occurs when a majority of the does in the local population begin approaching the zenith of their estrus cycles.

North of the Mason-Dixon line, this surge in mating activity occurs sometime during the month of November, with the exact time depending upon latitude and moon phase. In northern Michigan, for example, the rut peaks approximately November 5, while on my own home hunting grounds in southern Ohio it peaks about November 13.

The farther south, the more extended or protracted the rut becomes, due to the combined influences of more stable late-season weather patterns and the stimulating effects of photoperiodism, in which the daily length of sunlight is not as dramatically curtailed as it is farther north. If there is any discernible peak of the rut across the belt of southern states stretching from Florida to Texas, it generally occurs sometime during the last week of December and first two weeks of January.

Obviously, no matter where a hunter lives, timing is a crucial element in rut-hunting success. So he'll want to talk with a biologist, or study Murray's moon charts or Laroche's Rut Predictor, in order to peg the date the rut peaks in the specific region he plans to hunt.

Moreover, since moon phases and other factors change over time, these calculations must be done each year. To illustrate the variability involved, consider the state of Illinois, which spans a distance of more than 350 miles from its northern border with Wisconsin to its southern tip adjacent to Kentucky and Missouri. On average, the peak of the rut in southernmost Pulaski County may occur as much as ten full days later than in northernmost Winnebago County, and when moon phases are taken into account, this statewide variability from north to south may be as much as fourteen days.

While the peak of the first rut is unquestionably the most exciting time of year to scrape hunt, keep in mind that the mating period actually spans an approximate two-week period. This is because whitetail does, like human females, are individuals that do not cycle on precisely the same dates. Consequently, once the peak of the rut has been ascertained, a hunter can expect a certain percentage of does in his region to begin entering their estrus cycles at least a full week prior to the peak, while still other deer may not go into heat until a full week after the peak.

The significance of this is that many hunters do not hunt as seriously as they should prior to the peak of the rut, and once the specific peak rutting date has passed, they figure everything from that point on is strictly downhill.

THEY'RE DOING IT AGAIN

In going back to my sighting of the two bucks fighting over a doe long after the rutting period supposedly ended, that was the season I learned about the second rut.

The second rut can be partly attributed to Mother Nature's intended design that all creatures successfully reproduce. Yet due to a variety of biological reasons, many does bred by bucks do not conceive. As a result, it is nature's decree that these particular animals experience follow-up estrus cycles approximately twenty-eight days later as insurance that as many does as possible will be carrying fawns into the spring.

The intriguing thing about all of this is that mankind is also partly responsible for whitetails exhibiting more than one go-around at mating.

According to the laws of nature, harmony in the animal world means a balanced sex ratio of one female for every male. Yet for many generations, mankind upset this scheme by protecting does and harvesting bucks only. It has only been in the past decade that wildlife management has taken quantum leaps forward and we've come to recognize the importance of harvesting both bucks and does.

Yet many regions of the country have been slow to recover, quite often as a result of hunters continuing to refuse to take does; some hunters even apply for doe permits so that they can tear them up in a misguided belief the female of the species must be protected. When this happens, the does begin to far outnumber the available bucks to service them. I know of several regions where the sex ratio is twenty-five does to every one buck, a serious imbalance that means many of the does are not successfully impregnated each year.

To compensate for this violation of nature's intent, those still unbred does come into heat a second and even a third time late into the winter.

Unfortunately, when well-intentioned hunters and their state wild-life departments attempt to protect does, and thus create a great sex-ratio imbalance, they are actually harming their deer herds. Particularly in the northern states, deer that are commanded by their hormonal surges to engage in physically taxing mating activities late in the season often become so stressed and physically depleted that they are unable to survive the ravages of deep winter. Moreover, in the case of does, their fawns (if they survive) will be born so late the following summer that many of them may not have time to grow and achieve the necessary body weight to see them through their first winter.

SECONDARY BREEDING

The occurrence and intensity of additional rutting periods depends entirely upon the sex ratio of the herd. In a very few select regions of the country where the whitetail herd is in perfect balance—that is, where there is one buck for every doe—there is no second rut because 99 percent of the does are successfully bred during the first, or primary, breeding phase.

Consequently, secondary rutting periods characteristically occur in those regions where the buck to doe ratio is at least 10:1 and a third rut can be expected to occur where the buck to doe ratio is at least 20:1.

One tip-off of herd imbalance has to do with not only sighting far greater numbers of does than bucks but also observing fawn sizes in the spring and summer. In fact, not long ago I was talking with a local biolo-gist and happened to remark that for a number of years I had been seeing lots of unusually tiny fawns on my farm during July and August. I became worried they weren't getting enough to eat.

"Those fawns that appear so little are late-born deer," he explained. "Normally, when does conceive during the first rut in November, they drop their fawns the following May. But your deer population is growing so rapidly that the bucks are not able to service all of the available does during the first rut. As a result, many of them are conceiving later, during the second rut, and not dropping their fawns until June or July."

Clearly, I needed to do three things to enhance the health of my deer population: enlarge the existing food plots I already have in place, and consider new food choices that mature in summer and fall; begin a temporary, supplemental winter feeding program to help the stressed deer and underweight fawns make it through the next several winters; and immediately begin reducing the doe numbers to nip their population explosion in the bud.

DATING YOUR RUT HUNTING

All of this aside, it's worth emphasizing that most hunters simply are not aware of the late rutting that may be taking place in their regions. A high doe-to-buck ratio, as I discovered, is a sure indication. So is the spotting of what appear to be smaller than usual fawns during summer scouting missions.

A biologist associated with your state game department can undoubtedly provide even more accurate information regarding the sex ratio of the state's whitetail population. Then, it's easy to determine the date when you can expect to experience rut-hunting action a second and perhaps even a third time.

The important thing to remember is that a doe which does not conceive during her first estrus cycle will come back into heat twenty-eight days later. Yet keep in mind, as noted earlier, that a certain percentage of does can be expected to come into heat a full week prior to the peak of the rut, while still others may not enter estrus until a full week after the peak. So when post-dating, don't add twenty-eight days to the peak of the primary rut but to the onset of the breeding period, which begins about seven days earlier.

To illustrate the easy mathematics involved in this, consider a state where the primary rutting period peaks on November 15. Therefore, some does will begin entering their estrus cycles around November 8. By adding twenty-eight days to this date, you can be relatively certain that a second rut will begin on or about December 6, that it will reach its peak of intensity about December 13, and that some does will still be coming into estrus as late as December 20.

SCRAPING UP A BUCK

If there is a single drawback to hunting the second rut, it is that the bucks are generally a bit lethargic. The previous weeks of the primary breeding period have taken their toll, and those bucks that were not harvested are understandably gaunt and tired because a mature breeding buck can lose up to twenty percent of his body weight during the primary mating period.

Moreover, throughout the northern states, the weeks following the primary breeding period are usually characterized by colder and more unsettled weather. This means that wildlife is beginning to shift priorities to one thing: survival. The focus is on food and cover, and on conserving body heat and energy.

In the week prior to the peak of the second rut, hunt the same primary scrapes that produced buck sightings during the first breeding phase. Bucks will

A second rut occurs twenty-eight days after the conclusion of the first rut. It happens in those regions where there are too many does for the bucks to service during the first rut.

re-open those specific scrapes as they are visited by still-unbred does, but you can hasten a buck's re-visitation by dribbling doe-in-heat scent onto the scrapes.

If you found a good number of primary scrapes during the first rutting period, make a special effort during the second rut to hunt those particular scrapes located close to bedding and feeding areas. The bucks are now feeding more heavily to regain valuable lost body weight before deep winter arrives. Additionally, they are also spending more time bedding and resting, to reduce their body metabolisms so that maximum amounts of their food intake can be transformed into accumulated fat stores.

As the second rut peaks, bucks may continue revisiting their primary scrapes nearest their bedding and feeding grounds, but they become even more inclined to troll their home ranges and revisit their boundary scrapes.

This is exactly the opposite of what takes place during the primary breeding phase. During the first rut, such a large number of does come into estrus that a buck generally does not have to travel extensive distances to advertise for business. With such a large percentage of hot does, he's able to cling to the safety of the heavy-cover core areas of his home range, periodically check his closest primary scrapes, and enjoy all the female companionship he can handle.

But as the season wanes, and the second rut gets underway, a far smaller percentage of does comes into the secondary estrus cycle, and a buck has to travel farther and wider if he's to find serviceable does.

During the second, and even the third if I'm in a region where one occurs, I prefer to hunt those primary scrapes located closest to bedding

When a second rut is about to begin, bucks re-open many of their former primary scrapes. Since bucks are now still recuperating from the rigors of the first rut, hunt those primaries closest to thick bedding cover.

and feeding areas. But if those primaries do not appear to be vigorously tended, checking the former boundary scrapes may pay off.

One hunter I know accomplishes this as quickly as possible by dressing lightly in a jogging suit and wearing tennis shoes. He lopes along at a comfortable pace and is usually able to cover two or three miles of terrain during the early morning hours when he's not sitting on stand; if he finds one or two outlying scrapes that are steaming fresh, he quickly relocates his stand for the midday hunt.

What? This guy scouts for scrapes early in the morning and then hunts them during the afternoon?

Right! And this is perhaps one of the most valuable tips to keep in mind regarding the second rut. As the winter season progresses, the circadian rhythm of deer (their activity level) changes. As a result, with each

As winter approaches, the circadian rhythm of deer changes, causing them to be most active during midday rather than at dawn and dusk. Keep this in mind when hunting a second or third rut.

passing week they become less and less active during the morning hours and increasingly more active during midday.

In fact, one study conducted by biologist Larry Marchington at the University of Georgia revealed that, north or south, the peak activity level of the second rut occurs just before two o'clock in the afternoon! Consequently, it's best to spend the morning hours scouting, or staging drives for bedded deer, and to devote the midday hours sitting on stand in the vicinity of scrapes.

RATTLING AND GRUNTING

An overwhelming majority of hunters concentrate their antler rattling and grunting efforts upon the first rutting season. But according to noted Montana hunter Dick Idol, these two techniques may actually prove more effective weeks later, during the second rut, and they can be especially lethal in those particular locales that experience a third rut.

The reason once again hinges upon the fact that during the primary rut, a large percentage of the doe population is in estrus. This means that most bucks are almost continually in the company of one hot doe or another. When amorous bucks are exhibiting this so-called tending bond, you can rattle and grunt your heart out with little likelihood of persuading the bucks to leave the side of their lady friends. This is most notably the case with higher-ranking, dominant animals, which have proclaimed their right to do most of the breeding.

During the second rut, with most of the does in the region having already been successfully impregnated, there is less chance that a given buck will be enjoying female companionship. And during the third rut, there is even less likelihood the two will be paired up.

As a result, during the second and third rutting periods, any buck within earshot of antler rattling or grunting can easily be fooled into thinking that a still-unbred doe is experiencing a recurring estrus cycle, and that she's willing to be serviced, and that two other bucks are already on the scene. If he's a dominant buck in the local hierarchy, he'll rush to the scene to settle the dispute on his own behalf. But even if he's a subordinate buck, he's likely to approach in the hopes that, while the two superior animals are attempting to settle their differences, he might be able to sneak off with the hot doe himself.

Of course, none of this is meant to imply that the second rut, and especially the third rut, can ever be expected to measure up to the frenzied action that typifies the primary breeding period. The first rut is like Saturday night at a single's bar. That's when your chances of scoring are best. But if you strike out, the ballgame isn't over. There's more action to come, and it's scheduled to begin in about twenty-eight days.

Many experts believe rattling and grunting are more effective during the second rut than the first.

Chapter 8

Deer Are Where They Eat

It was the late commentator Earl Nightingale who once observed, "nature is not capricious . . . nature does not on the one hand give us the ability to clearly visualize a goal without at the same time giving us the ability to achieve it."

Translated into deer-hunting lingo, this means that one distinct advantage humans have in trying to outsmart whitetails is the superior ability to think and reason. Deer simply react, either by instinct or by utilizing rudimentary memory processes based on an ingrained desire to survive. But we can analyze, decipher, and plan.

In no other aspect of deer hunting does this more clearly come into play than learning which specific foods deer prefer most, scouting to find their locations, setting up a strategic ambush point, and then patiently waiting until the animal predictably makes its appearance.

The paradoxical thing about all of this, according to South Carolina whitetail authority Dr. Jim Casada, is that adult humans customarily eat their dessert last, at the end of a meal. Deer, on the other hand, are like children in that they always seek out dessert foods first. In fact, if the opportunity arises, they'll eat nothing but dessert!

A classic study conducted at Ohio State University's School of Agriculture, with the cooperation of other agricultural schools throughout the whitetail deer's native range, identified 614 types of plant life the animals were known to at least occasionally feed upon. The study emphasized that although deer are opportunists when it comes to feeding, they focus their daily lives upon a much smaller number of so-called "dessert foods," riveting their attention upon them until they're either depleted or past their prime in palatability.

KNOW YOUR HUNTING GROUNDS

Even though deer are tied to their favorite foods, the problem faced by hunters is that many of these foods (both native and domestic) exist only in certain regions. For example, in Vermont, September's main attraction may be apples. Yet in the October brush country of south Texas it may be a shrub known as huajilla, which possesses feathery, multiple-leaf fronds. And in Kentucky, where November's mountain ridges find themselves carpeted with acorns, you may see so many deer parading back and forth it's amazing they don't bump into each other.

So the important thing is your evaluation and interpretation of the area you will be hunting, and one of the best ways to begin is by consulting with an agronomist or botanist associated with your county extension agency, local technical college, or division of wildlife.

Scientists have determined that there are 614 types of plant life and other foods that deer consume on a regular basis.

Whomever you make contact with, show him the list of preferred deer foods presented in the sidebar accompanying this report and ask which ones are prevalent in your region, and under what kinds of soil or terrain conditions they usually grow so you can locate them when you're scouting.

Of course, I won't insult an advanced deer hunter's intelligence by presuming he cannot identify common foods such as acorns. But how many of us can readily identify horseweed, witch hazel, or staghorn sumac, among others, which deer will revisit every day if it is available? (Incidentally, staghorn sumac, which is recognizable by its twisted, disfigured branches and bright red seed clusters, is especially favored by deer during bitter cold winter months because the plant is exceptionally high in fat content and, when digested, helps deer generate body heat.)

Moreover, even when it comes to mast-bearing oak trees, deer much prefer the acorns of some oak species over others; some acorns are sweet and tender, but others are largely shunned by deer because they're high in bitter-tasting tannic acid or they're encased in caps that have sharp, spiny edges.

To illustrate how complicated proper acorn identification can be, let me introduce the following oak species: northern red oak, scarlet oak, shumard oak, pin oak, black oak, southern red oak, nuttal oak, blackjack oak, water oak, laurel oak, willow oak, live oak, white oak, swamp white oak, chestnut oak, bur oak, swamp chestnut oak, post oak, chinkapin oak, and overcup oak. That's twenty different species of acorn-bearing trees, some of which deer consider to be ice cream foods while others are rarely touched, and I've only listed those particular oaks found east of the Mississippi! (Incidentally, the three favorite acorns of whitetails come from the swamp chestnut oak, white oak, and pin oak).

Consequently, in addition to talking with a local agronomist or botanist, I strongly suggest every hunter also obtain a pocket-sized manual of trees and plants, with color identification pictures, for ready reference in the field.

In evaluating suspected feeding sites, keep in mind that other critters may be utilizing the same food sources and you don't want to mistakenly attribute their feeding signs for those of deer. Three examples are worth noting as a means of emphasizing the importance of this.

When you find small fragments of acorn shells, it's probably the work of squirrels, not deer. In the case of large acorns such as the swamp chestnut oak, deer crush the shells longitudinally into large halves or thirds; in the

A tree and plant guidebook taken afield will allow
you to identify the favorite foods of whitetails.

case of small acorns such as overcup or laurel oaks, deer spit out the caps
and swallow the small nuts whole, so there are no broken shell fragments—
just caps—laying on the ground. When you find ears of corn with just the
tender tip bitten off, it's the work of raccoons, not deer; deer nibble randomly upon the entire ear. And when you find low vegetation sheared off
cleanly, it's the work of rabbits; deer have a rough-textured "grinding pad"
in their mouths, and every sign of foraging on various species of vegetation
has a ragged and torn appearance.

GROW YOUR OWN TROPHY BUCKS

Is there any particular domestic (planted) food deer universally favor over
all others? The answer is a resounding yes! According to test results by the
Whitetail Institute of North America (WINA), the vegetation preferred
most by deer is a new type of ladino clover blend known, not coinciden-
tally, as Imperial Whitetail Brand Clover.

The Institute employs research agronomists and well-known deer biologists, and serves as a clearinghouse of information devoted exclusively to the white-tailed deer. According to WINA, this newly developed clover blend is certain to revolutionize deer hunting because it improves the overall quality of the species and greatly enhances antler growth.

I thought about that remark last season as I looked down upon a small food plot from a nearby tree stand. Below me were four does and two bucks, and whenever they periodically turned at just the right angle to the early morning sunlight, their coats glistened like neon signs. Even more impressive, both bucks sported larger antlers than we customarily see in southeastern Ohio.

"The reason the deer appeared to shine was because of lanolin in their coats," biologist Larry Weishuhn explained, "and this, along with the larger than average antlers, was due to an abundance of body mineral the deer couldn't have obtained from their usual native forage alone."

In recent years, Ray Scott of WINA, Larry Weishuhn, and many others have been intently studying the dietary needs of deer, and the conclusions they've reached are startling the outdoor world. "When deer are forced to get by with whatever nature provides, they are continually in a survival mode," Weishuhn explained. "But when hunters and landowners enter the picture and begin providing deer with plenty of extras, trophy bucks are the result."

To satisfy their nutritional needs, whitetails require about seven pounds of bulk food intake per day. Yet the big mistake made by hunters and landowners is providing this sustenance, often in the form of food plots, only in the spring and summer when deer need help the least. Instead, they should be setting the table for deer during the worst of times.

This is important, because it must be remembered that nutritional intake goes first to meet basic survival needs of an individual deer. It is only after these requirements are met do excess nutrients find themselves channeled into fawn development, antler growth, and resistance to diseases. Now you know why does in a given region sometimes have only single fawns while most of the bucks have thin, spindly antlers; the previous winter was particularly hard on them, and their body metabolisms commandeered virtually all spring and summer nutrient intake just to return them to a state of normal body health.

Consequently, when a given region is not producing large numbers of deer, and few quality bucks, it is almost always because nutritional foods are available there only on a seasonal basis.

The forage grasses most attractive to deer are alfalfa, ladino clover, red clover, white clover, bird's-foot trefoil, lespedeza, orchard grass, and timothy.

"This is exactly why I got involved in the development of Imperial Whitetail Brand Clover," Scott says. "It's an exciting deer food that will make the dreams of hunters come true wherever it is planted. The reason is because most quality grass forages used for hay production (such as alfalfa, orchard grass, and timothy) offer a 16 to 18 percent protein content, but the clover blend we designed offers an average of 25 to 30 percent protein."

Even more significant, and this goes back to our earlier mention of the importance of deer receiving highly nutritional food on a year-round basis, Imperial Whitetail Clover does not turn "woody" and stemmy in late summer and does not brown-out and go dormant in winter like other grass forages. Rather, it remains green, tender, and succulent twelve months a year throughout the US and Canada. Moreover, it adapts to a wide range of soil conditions and does not require annual reseeding.

"As far as palatability, deer prefer Imperial Whitetail Brand Clover five-to-one over livestock grasses," says Scott. "On our research grounds, the clover literally sucks deer out of surrounding regions. They walk right through other food plots to reach it."

What is even more astounding than Imperial Whitetail Brand Clover's ability to draw deer from afar is the effect it has upon antler growth. On WINA's research grounds, where deer had the opportunity to dine upon this unique clover blend over a brief period of only four years, spike bucks entirely disappeared! Every eighteen-month-old buck sporting his first antlers had a 6-point rack or better.

The reason for these incredible results is easy to explain. When deer are nutritionally well-fed on a year-round basis, they do not find themselves subjected to a spring recovery period. There's no required bounce-back time to compensate for winter's toll. This means that when spring arrives, does may immediately get on with the business of birthing and nursing healthy twins and triplets, and bucks may immediately begin laying down a foundation for heavy antler growth.

Imperial Whitetail Brand Clover, at a seed cost of about $82 per acre, is not expensive, and this makes it an ideal food-plot planting project for individuals or hunting clubs. The seed is now available through seed and farm supply dealers, as well as Amazon.com.

MORE GOOD EATS

"Although a high-protein diet is essential for healthy deer and the production of big antlers, other considerations also enter the picture," biologist Weishuhn asserts. "I recommend hunters maintain diversified foot-plot plantings, which is especially important in regions where there is competition from livestock that may be utilizing the same foods."

While Imperial Whitetail Clover is undoubtedly the ideal all-round food for deer, whitetails do not restrict themselves to just one food type if it is available year-round; the only time such focused attention is given to one type of food is when it is both high on their hit list and available for only a few weeks each year, such as in the case of acorns. Otherwise, in adhering to their instinctive need to evade predators, whitetails distinctly prefer buffet-style eating, in which they can nibble upon a little of this and a little of that as they remain constantly on the move.

As a result, hunters who own land, or have leased lands, or have close relationships with farmers, should offer their deer a smorgasbord of good eating. This means planting a variety of other items as well.

"I recommend hunters establish two types of food plots," says Weishuhn. "One should specifically consist of winter foods to help animals through a period of great physiological stress. Ideal foods to plant include oats, winter wheat, triticale, or Austrian winter peas. Corn is also a great food because of its high carbohydrate content, but since corn requires heavy-duty farm equipment to plant, it's faster and less expensive to simply buy several rows of corn from a large field a farmer has planted and tell him to leave it standing.

"Late spring and early summer food plots are also necessary," Weishuhn continues, "because during this period deer likewise are subjected to high nutritional needs. Does must give birth to healthy twins, nurse them, and then wean them onto nutritional solid foods. Meanwhile, bucks are experiencing the critical developmental stages of antler growth. In these food plots, I recommend hunters plant sorghum, hilgari, alfalfa, soybeans, or summer peas."

PLANTING TIME

Many hunters shy away from planting nutritious foods to help their deer because they have misconceptions about food plots. Let's clear the air by saying that establishing several food plots does not require a lot of acreage, the project does not require a tremendous amount of hard work, you don't need much in the way of equipment, and the financial investment is small compared to other routine hunting expenses.

Take my own 170-acre research farm in southeastern Ohio. I have two seven-acre meadows planted to Imperial Whitetail Clover. In both cases, a neighbor farmer plowed, disked, and planted the ground at a cost of $30 per hour (the work took two days).

Yet I also have numerous one-quarter-acre food plots in alfalfa, oats, wheat, and soybeans. My total cash outlay for these food plots came to less than $100 (for seed, fertilizer, and lime); the time involved in preparing the four sites and planting the seeds amounted to roughly two days; and the equipment was no more sophisticated than the rototiller and assorted hand tools I use in my vegetable garden every year.

In steep hollows and other rough areas where machinery of any type cannot be used, I've hand-planted still more acreage to Japanese honeysuckle; this is a vinelike plant that spreads rapidly, remains green and palatable year-round, and also affords excellent security cover. No cost was involved, because I simply used cuttings taken from plants existing elsewhere.

Hunters who own or lease land can attract deer by putting in food plots. Those on a tight budget can use common garden equipment to put in smaller food plots.

Since deer are creatures that like to keep on the move while eating, food plots should not be overly large; six or seven acres is the maximum recommended size. Whenever possible, make these food plots easily accessible to deer by situating them in clearings in forestland cover. Although my two seven-acre food plots are larger than normal, each of them, and also the small one-quarter-acre food plots, are surrounded on all sides by deep woodland cover. This accomplishes two things. First, it encourages and allows deer to utilize the food undisturbed during all hours of the day; otherwise, they'd be inclined to visit the food only at night. Second, as a direct result of the first, during hunting season you can sneak-hunt or sit on stand in the vicinity of your food plots.

Incidentally, still another attribute of Imperial Whitetail Brand clover is that it flourishes in semi-shaded areas. So reserve this particular food for your deepest woodland regions, and plant your other selected foods in areas that receive greater daily sunlight exposure.

As to actual planting techniques, establishing food plots is not difficult because the seeds are small and do not need to be covered with more than one-half inch of soil. As noted above, when putting in small food plots, I use my garden tiller to quickly rough-up the ground. The seeds can then be sowed by broadcasting (throwing small handfuls) or by using a shoulder-bag seeder for a more even distribution. Next broadcast handfuls of fertilizer such as 12–12–12 or triple-13. Finally, drag the backside of a rake over the ground to lightly cover the seed and fertilizer.

VARIETY IS THE SPICE OF A DEER'S LIFE

Because establishing food plots has proven to be so beneficial to all wildlife species, many state game departments and local conservation agencies are now offering "wildlife seed packets" to the public. These two-pound seed packets are usually free, the only requirement being that you must own or lease a minimum of five acres of land. If you don't own or lease land, you can obtain the same seed packets for a very nominal price and then plant the seeds (with permission) on the private land where you hunt.

The contents of these packets may vary between states in accordance with different climatic and soil conditions, but in all cases they contain a wide assortment of seeds that will germinate into plants favored by deer and other wildlife species. The most recent packets I obtained and planted contained seeds that later resulted in diverse food plots containing sunflowers, millet, corn, orchard grass, rye, soybeans, bird's-foot trefoil, red clover, oats, blackberries, and some other plant varieties I couldn't identify.

MINERAL MAGIC

I also strongly suggest providing deer with some type of mineral supplement. Numerous studies have shown that mineral supplements in excess of what is naturally available in any habitat will produce positive, often dramatic results in antler size and herd reproduction.

These supplements are available in block and granular form, but since there are so many brands on the market, many hunters are confused as to which is best.

"In conjunction with Purina Mills, I've recently been involved in a variety of whitetail deer research projects dealing with nutritional aspects

Deer are attracted and held in areas when they have a variety of prime foods, so don't plant just one thing.

Establishing mineral licks is inexpensive and deer actually paw depressions to obtain every bit. Whenever rainwater fills the depression, they gulp down the enriched beverage.

of the species," biologist Weishuhn recently told me. "I had friends from across the whitetail's broad range send me freshly shed antlers, including some really big ones. We then took core samples from these antlers and analyzed them for their primary composition."

What Weishuhn discovered was that the bigger antlers were much higher in sodium, zinc, and manganese than the other antlers. So good advice is to read the ingredients labels on any mineral supplement you're considering, to learn which particular brands are highest in the above elements.

Although mineral supplements are marginally expensive, especially if you buy them in twenty-five-pound blocks or fifty-pound bags of granules and have them mailed to you, they go a long way. You need only one so-called "mineral lick" for every forty acres of deer habitat, and under normal conditions each lick needs to be "sweetened" with a re-application only once every two or three years.

One word of advice. Hunting over a mineral block may be illegal in some states, so check your regulations booklet. It's usually a waste of time, anyway, because the most frequent visitation by deer is during the spring and summer, when a buck's antlers are in the developmental stage and does are lactating, and both have a need for maximum mineral intake. These needs don't exist in the fall and winter, so visits to mineral licks are infrequent then.

NATIVE FOODS DEER PREFER MOST

red maple	white cedar
aspen	juniper
pinyon pine	dogwood
witch hazel	swamp chestnut oak (acorns)
poplar	white oak (acorns)
osage orange	pin oak (acorns)
huajilla	greenbrier
staghorn sumac	wintergreen
mountain maple	hemlock
arbutus	ash
honeysuckle	willow
horseweed	crabapple
persimmon	beech (beechnuts)
honey locust	paw-paw

DOMESTIC FOODS DEER PREFER MOST

Imperial Brand Whitetail Clover

soybeans	corn
alfalfa	apples
red clover	white clover
rye grass	lespedeza
winter oats	trefoil
cabbage	carrots
blackberry	blueberry
elderberry	cranberry
lettuce	sugar beets
winter wheat	triticale
summer peas	Austrian winter peas
sorghum	hilgari

Chapter 9

Find Your Way, Find Your Deer

There was a time in our collective history as deer hunters when toilet paper served two purposes. One of those needs was flagging a trail to one's stand or a downed deer, but it was not without disadvantages; it would blow away, deteriorate in rain, and become obscured from view at night or when sudden snow draped the forest's limb work.

Since deer hunters commonly travel to and from their stands in darkness, often in unfamiliar country, it's essential they learn fail-safe ways of getting around.

But today, a wadded-up roll of tissue in one's pocket fulfills only its second function because there are now a variety of electronic aids that enable hunters to do their thing in the outback. These days, discovering the whereabouts of bucks worth hunting, finding the way to a stand and then back to camp, and recovering downed deer, have all become remarkably easy, even in unfamiliar terrain or in pitch darkness.

THE GPS BREAKTHROUGH

Incredibly, when a hunter establishes a link with overhead satellites, he can easily hike right to his tree stand in the deep woods in pre-dawn darkness, even if it's a winding route through several miles of nearly impenetrable cover. Later that evening, when darkness has settled in, he can unerringly find his way back to his vehicle, even taking a different route if he had to leave his stand to track an animal. Then, still later, back at car or camp, after he has enlisted the aid of several partners to help drag, he can lead them back to his downed deer, taking perhaps still a different route to a location that may be some distance from his stand.

The hi-tech wizardry that accomplishes all of this for the hunter is a lightweight Global Positioning System (GPS) unit.

Elsewhere, another hunter might plug the same type of hand-held unit into his 4WD's cigarette lighter socket, or use a larger, permanently mounted vehicle unit, to wend his way through a huge national forest's confusing network of criss-crossed dirt roads to find the specific turn-off where he previously located a hot scrape line.

Of course, neither example presented here eliminates the need to acquire woodsman's skills, because the hunter must still be able to scout, analyze sign, and have a knowledge of deer behavior. But with a GPS unit he can reduce his time-consuming reliance upon map and compass work, neither of which are much fun to use in darkness or sour weather. And he can venture far off the beaten track to explore new areas with the confidence that his battery-operated guide can show him the shortest route back to his starting point.

HOW GPS WORKS

The GPS navigational network was developed for the United States Department of Defense primarily as a military targeting and navigational system that drew acclaim during Desert Storm maneuvers in the Middle East.

GPS is now available to the general public in a downsized version. Based upon a constellation of twenty-four satellites orbiting the earth, GPS operates twenty-four hours per day, in any weather conditions, anywhere in the world. These satellites transmit high-frequency radio signals to the earth's surface, where a GPS receiver locks in on them. The receiver then triangulates from three satellites to provide latitude, longitude, altitude, and other navigational data. This allows a hunter's present position to be updated continuously, as well as his speed, direction of travel, and destination.

It should be mentioned that since GPS is owned and operated by the Department of Defense, the satellites beam two types of coded signals back to earth. The first types are known as Standard Positioning System (SPS) signals, the others are Precise Positioning System (PPS) signals, and it shouldn't take a rocket scientist to figure out which signals can be received only by military units and which are received by civilian GPS units.

Nevertheless, manufacturers of GPS systems available to the public claim accuracy to within fifty feet, 95 percent of the time, to ranges extending from one-tenth of a mile to 1,000 miles, which is more than ample for deer hunters.

IN THE FIELD

Among advanced deer hunters, several of the more popular brand names of GPS units currently on the market are those made by Eagle Electronics, Garmen, Lowrance, and Magellan Systems. The pricing range is $99 to $350.

Let's say a hunter has driven down a long dirt road in a 100,000-acre national forest, made several turns, then parked in a pull-off and is ready to begin scouting for encouraging deer sign.

Before he leaves his vehicle, he turns on his GPS unit and gives it a moment to lock-in to three satellites and program his location. He's then free to wander through miles of real estate, concentrating upon finding evidence of deer sign. As the hours pass, he may find several different scrape lines, rub lines on heavily used trails, bedding areas, feeding areas, and other indications of deer activity.

Since the hunter knows that he may wish to return to each of these places to more closely investigate them, he logs location into his GPS unit.

He may even find spots for installing tree stands, not necessarily because of fresh sign in the vicinity but because they are places with natural funnels, escape hatches and other travel corridors. He consequently logs those locations into his GPS unit as well.

Companies that make GPS units call these logged-in references "waypoints," and some models have enough memory capacity to store up to 200 different event recordings.

Hours later, at the conclusion of his scouting mission, with the hunter now having no idea where his vehicle is parked, he "punches in" the starting location that he recorded earlier. His GPS unit then produces a graphic display map on its screen, with an arrow pointing him in the correct direction; as he hikes, the arrow moves slightly, continually informing him of needed course corrections.

Days later, perhaps after scouting other areas many miles away, the hunter may decide that a particular scrape line he located the first day is his hottest find, and that he wants to hang a stand there on opening morning. But since it was far back in the hinterland, he's not quite sure how to get there, especially in the dark.

No problem. He simply turns on his GPS unit, goes into its memory bank where the information is recorded, and punches in the particular waypoint; since it has a lighted screen, he can easily read it in the dark. Then he shoulders his stand, grabs his bow or gun, turns on his flashlight so he won't trip over a log, and begins hiking straight to the location. What could be easier?

"In addition to a variety of display information, our AccuNav Sport features ten special displays called 'Windows' which group different kinds of travel information into easy-to-read split panels," says Eagle's Tim Neece. "For example, one window will tell you how fast you're going, while another tells you how far you have to go. Another tells you the course bearing in which you're headed, while another tells you the direction you should be headed so you can make a slight correction in the direction you're hiking if you're not heading the right way."

Of course, this is only a distillation of the capabilities of a most GPS units. The new technology performs many other functions as well.

For example, in desiring to return to a particular stand location (a waypoint), you may not want to travel the same route you took the first time. After all, you may have randomly zig-zagged and wandered around for several hours before finding that stand site and you don't want to waste time retracing that exact route. Your GPS unit's screen will display both the original route you took, and the shortest route from your current location.

Or, let's say you and your partner leave your vehicle, and each of you head in different directions, to your respective stand sites. Before splitting up, you decide to rendezvous at some other location at midday to begin a two-man still-hunt. With the waypoint data logged into both of your GPS units, you can each leave your stand and hike directly to that agreed-upon meeting place with unerring accuracy.

The instruction manuals accompanying each GPS unit describe many other functions as well, enabling today's advanced deer hunter to find his or her way around in the outback almost as well as the deer themselves!

PRIVATE EYES

It was the late Earl Nightingale, of radio broadcast fame, who coined the phrase, "luck is what happens when preparedness meets opportunity."

Well, many modern hunters are making their own luck through the use of trail cameras. These devices solve the riddle of what time of day various trails are being used by deer, which is critically important because

Trail cameras can tell you which trails deer are most frequently using, and when.

some trails are reserved for daytime use while others are used exclusively after dark.

The standard way of using one of these battery-operated game clocks is to attach it to a tree trunk on one side of a trail. If an animal passes by, an infrared sensor will detect the body heat of deer walking down a trail, visiting scrapes, or entering a feeding area. It will then take photos or videos and record the date and time of each animal's presence in the area, from up to ninety feet away; there's no need to check the equipment every day because some models will record up to 1,000 separate events. Some models allow the hunter to select the height of the infrared beam so that unwanted animals (coyotes, raccoons, stray dogs, turkeys) are not recorded.

Since these deer surveillance devices use passive infrared technology, they can be programmed to photographically record deer in daylight, in full darkness, or both. Most devices also have delay mechanisms that prevent them from repeatedly photographing the same animal. They instead allow each animal to move out of the sphere of coverage before another photo is shot of the next animal that comes along.

Are these devices worth $200 to $600? Many hunters believe there is simply no better way to decide whether a scrape, rub-line or trail is worth hunting. With a combination unit that possesses a trail clock and camera, a hunter knows exactly when a deer is using a particular area. Of even more significance, he can examine his photos and see exactly what antler size the animal is carrying. If a hunter cannot afford several of these ingenious hunting aids, he might want to consider splitting the cost with regular hunting partners.

OTHER AIDS, TIPS, TRICKS

Every deer hunter should carry trail markers in his fanny pack. There are many styles on the market, the most popular being Limb Lights and Bright Eyes.

As accurate as a GPS unit is for getting you within forty or fifty feet of your stand, that may not be close enough if you've done a proper job of concealing your stand in a tree with plenty of gnarled limbs and perhaps even a branch strategically placed here and there. Many times I've had to pan my flashlight beam around in the blackness of night, wasting valuable time looking for my stand.

Now I look upon trail markers as something to be put into place for a distance of less than fifty yards. In other words, I use my GPS unit to reach the general area of my stand, then use trail markers to guide me to the stand itself. This lets me get in and out as quickly and as quietly as possible, without unnecessarily contaminating the surrounding ground cover with human scent.

Limb Lights are twist-ties of the type used to secure plastic bags, except that they have a reflective surface that glows brightly, with a complete 360-degree radius of reflection when a flashlight beam is shined in the general area. By tying a Limb Light to a tree limb every ten yards, you can actually create a glowing highway right to your stand. They can also be removed and used over and over again.

Bright eyes are simple thumbtacks with heads that have a coat of fluorescent paint. Like Limb Lights, they are virtually invisible in daylight (so you're not advertising the location of your stand to other hunters), but when illuminated by a flashlight create a virtual path to one's stand or ground blind.

BLOOD-TRAILING MADE EASY

When the sign peters out, what to do? Some hunters begin wandering around aimlessly, hoping to come upon crimson droplets at some other location. Trouble is, this is a hit-or-miss proposition that takes too much time and is often ineffective.

Photo courtesy of Fiduccia Enterprises.

Instead, try using the grid system of relocating sign when the blood trail runs out. By walking in ever widening rectangular patterns, chances are greatly increased that you'll find your animal.

Don't make the mistake of attempting to blood trail a deer after dark with a flashlight. The beam just isn't strong enough to adequately expose the tiniest droplets. If you can, use a kerosene or gasoline lantern or a seal-beam spotlight that casts a broad light over a wider area than a concentrated flashlight beam.

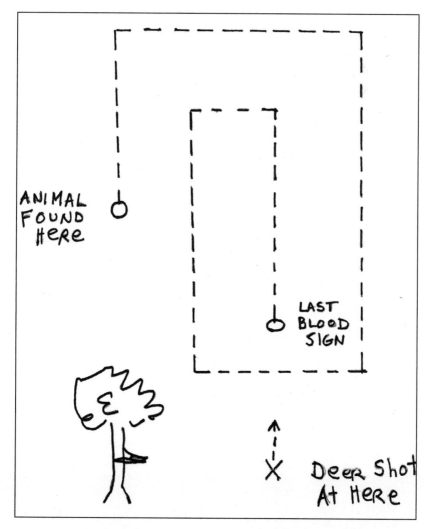

Lost your buck's blood trail? Use the age-old trick of hiking a methodical grid and eventually you'll find the blood trail again or the animal itself.

GETTING IT ALL TOGETHER

When using the grid system to relocate a blood trail that suddenly dwindled to nothing, pause every 100 yards or so. Pan the terrain in all directions and it may point straight toward the downed animal's location, thus ending your need to blood trail any farther. If not, continue hiking the rectangular grid for another 100 yards and then pan the terrain again.

Eventually, you're sure to recover your deer. But in executing so many turns while hiking the grid system, it's likely you'll have become disoriented and have no idea how to get back to camp or your parked vehicle, especially if it's dark or stormy.

No problem. You've got a guide in your pocket. Merely turn on your GPS unit, give it a minute to lock-in on several satellites, and it will momentarily tell you the exact way back to a crackling fireplace and hot toddy.

Chapter 10

Pick a Winning
Stand Area

The greatest impediment to taking a mature white-tailed buck is not being in the right place at the right time. In fact, the legendary Fred Bear once observed that "you can't shoot a deer you don't see."

Not long ago, when researching material for a series of magazine articles, I went straight to today's whitetail experts, hunting with them over the course of several years and picking their brains about their favorite stand-hunting hotspots. The advice I sought had to be relevant to bowhunters and firearm hunters alike, no matter where they live or hunt, and no matter whether they prefer to use portable tree stands or ground blinds.

The hunting luminaries I talked with earn their full-time livelihoods from deer hunting, and collectively have pursued trophy whitetails in every state inhabited by the species. The list included long-time friends Harold Knight and David Hale, owners of Knight & Hale Game Calls in Cadiz, Kentucky; Will Primos, owner of Primos Game Calls in St. Flora, Mississippi; Jim Crumley, owner of TreBark Camo in Roanoke, Virginia; Larry Frasier, head guide for Deer Creek Outfitters in Sebree, Kentucky; Johnny Lanier and Leo Allen, owners of Bent Creek Lodge in Jachin, Alabama; and Ray McIntyre, former owner of Warren & Sweat Tree Stands in Grand Island, Florida.

At the conclusion of this quest, I allowed my computer to digest the countless pages of interview notes. It coughed up seventeen different types of locations where a hunter can place a stand with expectations of taking a larger than average buck.

Incidentally, I also reflected back over three decades of hunting white-tails and, not surprisingly, I could recall taking bucks in every one of the expert's recommended locations. When you take your buck this year, I'll wager it will be in one of the following places.

MAJOR DEER RUNWAYS

"Major deer runways serve as travel corridors between bedding and feeding areas," David Hale said. "While a network of other threadlike trails may criss-cross the terrain, there is no mistaking a major runway. It may be quite wide, due to generations of deer repeatedly using this thoroughfare, and the soil will have become so compacted over the years that little vegetation grows there. Although a major deer runway may course through a tract of forest land, you're more likely to find it in conjunction with restrictive terrain features such as long, narrow hollows, lengthy streambottoms, or where distinctly different cover-types meet, such as pines bordering hardwoods."

Major deer runways reveal plenty of all-day deer traffic, but the only time bucks travel such runways is during the beginning of the rut when does are coming into heat.

According to Harold Knight, in fall and winter major deer runways are predominantly used by doe-family groups (one or two does, their most recent offspring, and perhaps a spike buck, forkhorn, or daughter from the previous season). Mature bucks use major deer runways only during the peak-rut phase of the mating period when they are engaging in trail-transference in order to follow does approaching the peak of their estrus cycles.

MINOR DEER TRAILS

"Minor deer trails are used by mature bucks during the non-rutting weeks of the fall and winter months," Will Primos told me. "Mature bucks do not like to associate with doe-family units at this time, preferring to keep their private lives private. Occasionally, you may find a minor deer trail paralleling a major deer runway on the runway's downwind side and in much heavier cover; this allows a buck to keep tabs on the activities of other deer and to even use them as sentries to forewarn him of danger."

Minor deer trails are predominantly buck trails, and they are commonly found running parallel to and downwind of major deer runways.

"However, in a majority of cases, mature bucks will adopt their own home-range areas away from doe-family groups," Jim Crumley added. "Minor deer trails can be difficult to identify because they are not tamped down to the same degree as major deer runways, and this allows vegetation to hide them from view in many places."

A very light skiff of snow on the ground makes the task of identifying such trails infinitely easier. Be especially alert for the absence of very small tracks. When small tracks are found in conjunction with large tracks, a doe-family unit is using the trail, not a lone buck.

SCRAPE CONCENTRATIONS

"A mature whitetail buck may create as many as three dozen scrapes during the pre-rutting period, but a majority of them are quickly abandoned and only a very few become elevated in status to primary scrapes," Larry Frasier explained. "Moreover, setting up in the vicinity of clusters of scrapes is generally far more productive than merely standing watch over a lone scrape, because the concentrated nature of the breeding sign indicates the animal's re-visitation on a far more frequent basis."

"What most hunters do not understand about the rutting period is that waiting on a stand near primary scrapes is most effective only during the pre-breeding phase of the rut, which is about two weeks before does reach the zenith of their estrus cycles," Jim Crumley said. "During the peak of the rut, scrape hunting continues to be effective, but a much wiser tactic is to occupy a stand overlooking a major deer runway or a doe-family bedding area because anxious bucks will be spending less time tending their scrapes and increasingly more time in the vicinity of does, waiting for the very first ones to become receptive."

TRAIL HUBS

A trail hub is where two or more trails cross. Intersecting major deer runways always reveal the most deer traffic (in the form of does, their current offspring, and immature bucks).

Conversely, intersecting minor deer trails reveal far fewer sightings of animals; however, since most of the animals sighted will be mature bucks, these are the places to search for during the non-rutting period.

"As the rut intensifies, a trail hub that produces day-long excitement with plenty of various-age animals sighted is a location where a minor deer trail, that is, a buck trail, intersects with a major deer runway being used by doe-family groups," David Hale emphasized. "Keep in mind that the greatest incidence of trail hubs occurs on relatively level terrain where the cover is of mixed species."

BOUNDARY TRAILS

A whitetail's home range averages less than two square miles in size, with the perimeter often delineated by major terrain features such as lakeshores, rivers, sheer rocky bluffs, deep gorges, and forest edges that yield to wide-open prairie land.

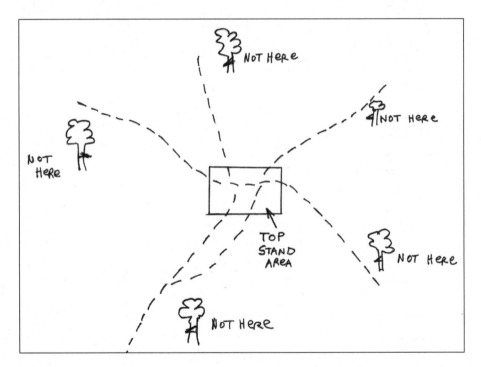

Trail hubs are places where two or more trails intersect. The best stand areas are those from which a hunter has shooting coverage to all of the trails.

"Scout these likely home-range boundary areas and you'll find trails" Johnny Lanier advised. "When deer are engaging in routine daily behavior, boundary trails are infrequently used. But if there are few does in the region and the rut is in progress, bucks will patrol boundary areas, covering many miles per day in search of estrus females."

"If hunting pressure mounts, bucks will filter out of their usual haunts to find seclusion in peripheral areas; now is when boundary trails also become hotspots worth watching," Leo Allen added.

ESCAPE TRAILS

"Under intense hunting pressure, and especially during the course of drives, deer immediately vacate their areas of normal activity and head for very heavy cover or difficult terrain," Will Primos observed. "Knowing this, and knowing in advance where that hunting pressure is likely to originate, such as from a campground or popular hunter parking area, watching an escape trail can pay handsome dividends."

"First, locate the most nightmarish cover you can find in the region," Larry Frasier suggested. "It might be a swamp or a spruce bog, but it could also be a ravine choked with brush and jackstrawed logs, a pine plantation, or a jungle of tall vegetation such as Phragmites or cane. Next, search for tracks entering the cover. If you can find tracks that are splayed and eight- to ten-feet apart, indicating a bounding animal, you've found an escape trail."

RUB LINES

"Essentially, a rub line indicates a minor deer trail used by a buck. But compared to a minor trail used by a buck on a year-round basis, a rub-line trail is used most frequently during the pre-rut period," Jim Crumley explained. "The foremost purpose of the trail is still a travel route back and forth between bedding and feeding areas, but it's fully within the area where the buck hopes to eventually breed and he is therefore inclined to mark it with visual and olfactory signposts. As the rut gets underway, a rub-line trail may also connect scrapes strung out across the countryside."

"A recent rub will reveal a moist, light-colored cambium, while one that is weeks old will have begun to dry and turn slightly gray in color," Harold Knight said. "I like to find rub lines where there are individual rubs that are very fresh, moderately old, and very old, as this indicates the animal is traveling that specific route on a regular basis, making it an ideal location for stand placement."

DOE-FAMILY BEDDING AREAS

Does and their most recent offspring generally bed in thickets or midway up sloping terrain, as opposed to bottomlands or along ridges. Just as it is possible to identify major deer runways used by doe-family groups by finding a combination of large and small tracks, an observant hunter can likewise be sure he has found a doe-family bedding area by the presence of both large and small matted ovals in grass, leaf litter, and snow, and seeing evidence of both large and small droppings.

"The prime time to hunt a doe-family bedding area is the pre-breeding phase of the rut, as amorous bucks will be nearby, anxiously waiting for the first does to enter estrus," David Hale noted. "A stand should be located at least 100 yards away from the actual bedding area, on a main trail leading toward it, to avoid getting too close and spooking the animals."

MATURE BUCK BEDDING AREAS

"Mature bucks generally bed higher than doe-family units and in thicker cover. Since mature bucks are usually solitary animals, the discovery of a lone bed in a region pockmarked with numerous rubs on saplings, and a combination of old and fresh tracks and droppings, is what you should be looking for," said Will Primos.

"There are two best times to wait on a stand near a mature buck bedding area," Ray McIntyre added. "The first is very early in the season, well before the pre-breeding period of the rut. The second is during the post-rut phase when exhausted bucks enter a week or more of recuperation and thus spend more time than usual in their bedding areas."

Of critical importance, remember that a mature buck's selection of a bedding area is based solely upon the feeling of safety offered by that place. If you violate the buck's security by installing your stand too close, he'll vacate the region and begin bedding elsewhere. All of my interview experts agreed that a hunter should set up at least 200 yards away from a mature buck's bedding area, on a minor deer trail leading from the bedding region to a prime food source, and he should occupy his stand only on those days when the wind is absolutely in his favor.

Mature buck bedding areas are difficult to hunt because one must never violate the resident buck's feeling of security or he'll leave, perhaps forever. Sometimes a quickie ground setup along a trail leading to the bedding area is less intrusive than hanging a tree stand.

GRAZING AREAS

Early in the season, before killer frosts wipe out lush vegetation, whitetails are primarily grazers. "Search for secluded grassy openings, hay meadows, soybean fields, and native species of greenery that deer in that region prefer. Then establish a stand that will allow you to watch the food site at morning's first light and again at dusk." Johnny Lanier advised.

Owing to their generally large sizes, grazing areas such as forage grasses, grainfields, and food plots are more efficiently covered by firearm hunters rather than bowhunters. Dawn and dusk are the best hunting times.

BROWSING AREAS

"As the season progresses and vegetation begins turning brown and entering a dormant state, whitetails become browsers and dote upon the tender twigs, buds, and branch tips of regenerative saplings and immature brush," Harold Knight said. "No matter where you live within the whitetail's range, you should be able to find either white cedar, red maple, mountain maple, or black ash, all of which deer browse upon heavily. Remember, the browse material must be within their reach, and this means finding immature trees with low branches no more than six feet off the ground."

ICE CREAM FOOD AREAS

In every region of the country, deer have certain foods that are special treats. Since these treats are usually available for only very brief periods, they draw animals from afar.

"Examples of these ice cream foods include the two- to three-week long acorn drop, the several week period in which orchard fruits are maturing, and fields containing crop-residue spillage immediately after corn, soybeans, carrots, and sugar-beets have been harvested," Ray McIntyre said.

"Occupy your stand early and late in the day, just prior to the arrival of a storm front or, best of all, immediately after the passage of several days of severely inclement weather," he concluded.

STAGING AREAS

"Staging areas consist of 100- to 200-yard-wide bands of thick cover sur-rounding grazing areas, browsing areas, or ice cream food areas," Will Primos explained. "If a given food site is relatively close to occupied dwellings or roads, deer will mill around in a staging area until darkness sets in before exposing themselves in the open to feed. The same is also true in secluded regions where hunting pressure is intense.

"After finding one of the three types of feeding areas that deer are fre-quenting, scout the adjacent cover for approach trails and place your stand at least fifty yards back in the cover so you'll be able to see your quarry before evening shooting light fades. Morning stands in staging areas might have to be as much as 100 yards from the actual food site because mature bucks often leave the open feeding grounds before dawn's shooting light arrives."

CLEARCUTS AND BURNS

When a forest fire ravages the terrain, everything looks charred and hor-rible for many months. However, ash deposits reduce the pH content of the soil, and what emerges is extremely succulent, high-quality, regenerative vegetation that draws deer from surrounding areas.

"When logging companies clear-cut a tract of climax forest, the elimi-nation of the trees likewise scars the landscape. Yet with the overhead, shade-producing canopy now eliminated, a profusion of ground-story plants and saplings emerges, providing deer with a cornucopia of feeding opportunities," Johnny Lanier said.

"Periodically check with your local Forest Service office or timber company to learn of recent forest fires or logging operations, and you'll undoubtedly find more deer per square mile in those regions than elsewhere."

STORMY-WEATHER BEDDING AREAS

Deer are relatively immune to the effects of precipitation, but when it occurs in conjunction with winds exceeding ten miles per hour, they hole up in protective cover. Every hunter should therefore have at least one stand overlooking a trail leading into or through a stormy weather bedding area.

"Because they retain their leaves year-round, conifers are the most favored stormy weather bedding sites," David Hale noted.

"In the absence of evergreens, look for walls," Harold Knight added. "These are the protected lee sides of thick cover such as multiflora rose, honeysuckle, brush, or steep boulder-riddled terrain, all of which have the effect of blocking the wind and thereby allowing an animal better use of his senses than elsewhere."

DIVERSION AREAS

"A diversion area is any natural terrain feature or manmade confluence that squeezes deer traffic in a certain direction," Larry Frasier observed. "An example of a natural diversion area might be a constricted bottleneck in a steep bottomland. A manmade diversion might be a permanently open gate in a fenceline.

"Also scout for narrow corridors through thick stands of cover, perhaps where a winding band of infertile soil has prevented lush natural growth, or even several blown-down trees which deer are likely to detour around."

CROSSINGS

"Next time you see a precautionary deer-crossing sign along the highway, pull over onto the berm and spend a few minutes studying your surroundings," Will Primos suggested. "Likely as not, you'll see that both sides of the road consist of long stretches of relatively open ground except for that one specific place where two opposing tracts of woodland closely border the road and that is precisely where the sign has been placed.

"Whitetails are cover-loving creatures, yet they regularly cross fields, meadows, pastures, and even highways during their travels. Naturally, they'll most often cross at a particular location where they need not expose themselves for any longer than necessary.

"So, when scouting, try to find a terrain situation that is similar to a highway deer crossing; that is, a piece of open ground where two opposing wooded points almost meet. When deer want to travel from the one woodlot to the other, their crossing location will undoubtedly be in the vicinity of the wooded points.

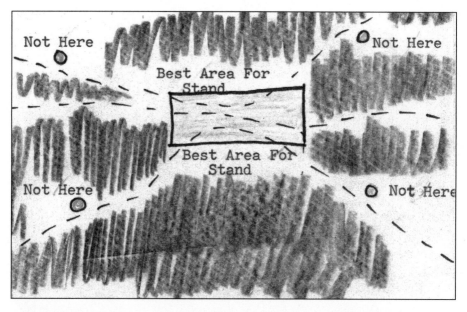

Diversion areas, sometimes also known as funnels or bottlenecks, force deer traffic to squeeze through a narrow area of terrain. Diversion areas are the most popular stand sites among bowhunters because of the generally short-range shots that are afforded.

"A low saddle crossing a steep ridge can also be a hotspot," Ray McIntyre advised. "In this case, however, it is not the cover per se that affords deer their needed sense of security, but the dip in the contour of the terrain so they are not silhouetted against the skyline."

"Another type of crossing I've found highly productive is a slightly elevated ridge of dry, wooded land separating two swamps," Will Primos said. "Spooked deer will not hesitate to bound away through standing swamp water, but unalarmed animals going about their routine business will consistently use the higher, drier ground instead."

DRINKING SITES

Under normal weather conditions, typical whitetail habitat has abundant "sheet water" in the form of streams, rivers, lakes, and springs. But deer are opportunists and will also drink from rainwater puddles, stock tanks, farmponds, roadside culverts, and irrigation ditches.

Consequently, drinking sites are not good places to establish stands under normal conditions when rainfall has adequately provided the animals with widespread drinking opportunities.

The prime time to sit on a stand near a drinking site is during a severe drought in which all but the largest sources of water are dry. Tracks peppering a drinking site tell you how many animals are visiting it, their frequency of visitation, and their probable sexes.

Drinking sites can be hotspots, but only during periods of severe drought when most of the local water sources are dried up.

The best time of day to occupy a stand near a water source is early morning, after the deer have concluded their daybreak feeding; conversely, in the evening, deer do not customarily show up at drinking sites until after full dark.

PICK OF THE LITTER

I've just described eighteen locations which, given the right time of year and/or certain weather conditions, are sure-fire places for taking a buck. Obviously, few of us have the time to place a stand in every one of the eighteen locations yet, at the other extreme, it would be unwise to put all your hope in only one stand.

A flexible hunter should probably have three to five different stand sites. This will allow him to adapt to changing conditions and also to rest each of his stands now and then, rather than burning out a single stand through continual use.

Of the eighteen stand locations described, it is imperative to have a stormy weather stand. Otherwise, whenever severe weather strikes, you might as well stay home because none of the other locations are likely to produce.

My second choice would be a trail hub, simply because part of the fun and excitement of deer hunting is seeing animals. By the same token, in being able to look over a number of different bucks, you stand a better chance of attaching your tag to something that is really exceptional.

A stand in a diversion area is essential if you live in a region where hunting pressure is light; if hunting pressure is intense, substitute an escape trail stand instead.

A stand overlooking a feeding area is a must. Make use of a portable stand for this type of work so you can easily relocate your stand from a grazing area to either a browsing area or ice cream food area as the season progresses.

Finally, my fifth stand choice would be near a mature buck bedding area, especially if the presence of a rub line, scrapes, or large tracks suggest that the deer in question is a trophy animal.

When scouting for bedding areas, remember two or three beds close to one large bed usually indicates it's where a doe with her offpsring have bedded. A single bed, usually on slightly higher ground, is more than likely that of a mature buck.
Photo: Ted Rose

Keep in mind when hunting the rut, that any doe that is not bred during the first rut, will come back into estrus during the next phase. She will continue to come into estrus every 28-30 days, for about three to four months, until she is successfully bred. Photo: Ted Rose

While a whitetail buck will attempt to mount an estrus doe all through the year, he is only capable of breeding her when his antlers are hardened and free of velvet. Photo: Ted Rose

This stand was built on the edge of a corn field with a thick staging area behind it where deer, especially bucks, mill around before coming to the corn. Photo: Fiduccia Enterprises

One way bucks check for any does in estrus, is to check the wind for estrus-laden scent. They breathe in air through their nostrils, curl their upper lips to close their nostrils, and then exhale through their mouths. As they exhale through their mouths, the scent passes by the vomeronasal organ which deciphers its contents. Photo: Ted Rose

The ratio of bucks to does affects the rut. In areas without many bucks, the rut is not intense as there are not enough bucks to breed all the does. In areas with a lot of bucks, the rut is frenzied as most of the does are bred in just a few days. Photo: Ted Rose

Rubs are olfactory signposts left by bucks to help establish a defined breeding area. When a buck rubs a larger tree, he is leaving a visual signpost as well. Photo: Fiduccia Enterprises

Many hunters examine deer pellets to determine whether they were left by a buck or a doe. Keep in mind that there are 30 different subspecies of deer and they vary greatly in body size and pellet size too. As long as you study pellets from one area and compare them, you can generally surmise that the larger pellets will come from bucks who are larger in body size than other deer. Photo: Ted Rose

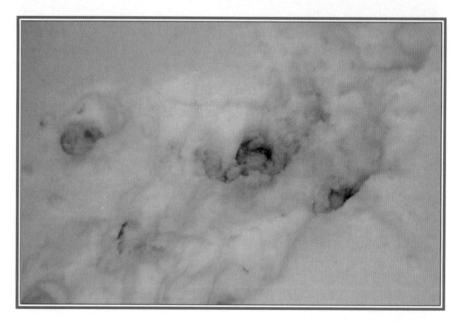

Finding urine along with deer tracks can tell you a few things. This urine was probably left by a doe who was squatting as she urinated. If it was left by a buck, it would be in front of the rear hoof marks and in a thin line. Also, if there was a bit of red in the urine, it would indicate this doe was in estrus. Photo: Fiduccia Enterprises

When examining deer tracks and looking for dew claw marks, remember both bucks and does have dew claws–and when the ground is soft, dew claw marks will be present in both their tracks. Photo: Fiduccia Enterprises

Deer are where they eat! This trail was planted with clover that grows well in the shade. Note the shooting house at the back of the trail. Photo: Fiduccia Enterprises

Rattling works anywhere there are whitetails. Keep in mind, the sound of antlers hitting each other is an integral part of the social structure of whitetails. Photo: Fiduccia Enterprises

Chapter 11

Fail-Safe Stand and Blind Set-Ups

Many firearms hunters believe that, since they're using a scoped rifle and can pop off a round at an unsuspecting animal up to 300 yards away, things such as scent drift or how deer catalog various sounds become virtually meaningless in terms of stand or blind placement.

But guess what? A recent hunter survey by the National Shooting Sports Foundation revealed that every year, the majority of firearm-killed deer are taken at seventy-five yards or less.

Consequently, I've always advised firearm hunters to use as much care in selecting their stands and blinds as bowhunters do. Who knows, even though your firearm may be capable of reaching way out there, the buck of your dreams may eventually step into view at a distance of only a dozen yards. And if he does, the smallest error in judgment or planning can become magnified to such proportions that it may easily cost you your prize. Actually, two types of error may enter the picture, for there are errors of omission (things we should have done but didn't) and errors of commission (things we did but shouldn't have). And it's usually the errors of commission that prove to be the most detrimental because, when the shooting distance is so close you can see a fly on the animal's coat, even the faint scratching noise of whisker stubble against your collar may send him crashing away through the brush.

That said, it's clear that one thing that distinguishes an advanced hunter is the degree of control he strives to maintain over his hunting and shooting set-ups. Much of this comes about through his learned ability to benefit from past experiences by remembering what worked well before and striving to duplicate those same circumstances time and again.

Bowhunters must select stand sites that afford close-range shots or deer will jump the string. Many experts believe eighteen yards is the ideal shooting range.

As a result, when describing "fail-safe" stand and blinds, I'm not referring to specific types of terrain locations as we did in the previous chapter, but attributes of stand and blind set-ups themselves. And to be sure, the higher the number of these desirable features that can be incorporated into a given stand location and its placement, the greater the hunter's chance of scoring.

NARROWING THE RANGE

Most bowhunting authorities agree that the ideal shooting range is somewhere between ten and twenty-five yards. Even though you may be capable of placing arrows accurately at thirty-five yards or beyond, it's not wise to shoot this far when hunting, due to a deer's ability to dodge the flight of the arrow.

Some hunters claim this is untrue, believing that arrows travel so fast, especially from modern compound bows, that it's virtually impossible for deer to "jump the string," but this is a huge misconception.

First, it is not the sight of the arrow flying toward them that deer react to, but the sound of the string being released. Even if you use string silencers such as cat-whiskers or acrylic yarn puffs, your string will still make a slight thud-like twang, which can cause a deer to instantly duck into a crouch. This is an instinctive reaction whereby a deer coils his legs like springs to propel him into an escape mode; a microsecond later, the arrow flies harmlessly over its back.

As far as arrow speed, most modern compound bows generally chronograph at around 250 feet per second. By comparison, sound travels at 1,088 feet per second. Therefore, noises made by you or your equipment will reach the deer five times faster than your arrow. What this means is that it takes a deer only three-tenths of a second to drop a full body size, but at twenty-five yards it takes your arrow at least five-tenths of a second to reach its target; hence, a clear miss. Yet, at eighteen yards or less, it takes an arrow only two-tenths of a second to reach its target; which means there's no chance for the deer to duck before the arrow arrives.

Obviously, many of us would probably be tempted to take a shot at a big buck beyond twenty-five yards. But if you keep in mind the rule of thumb of placing your stand within ten to twenty-five yards of where you expect to see deer, in the long run you'll experience far fewer misses. Then, if an occasional thirty- or thirty-five-yard shot does indeed present itself, and you can't resist taking it, remember to aim low—in the vicinity of the heart—so that when the animal predictably dives into a crouched position, he'll be moving downward into the arrow's flight path and you'll have a good hit in the lung region.

THE SUNLIGHT FACTOR

One error that both bow and gun hunters make is scouting during midday, when the sun is almost directly overhead, then completely overlooking the fact that, most probably, any shooting opportunity they're awarded will come early or late in the day when the sun is low on the horizon.

This reminds me of a hunt in Rockingham County, North Carolina. I was situated in what I thought was an ideal stand, watching a trail hub. As late afternoon approached and the sun began sinking to the horizon, it became increasingly more difficult to see the trail.

Then, just when the sun had become almost too blinding to look at, an impressive 10-pointer appeared. It was the biggest buck I had ever seen in this particular area, but by this time my burning eyes were squinted almost closed with stinging tears streaming down my face. With no choice, I slowly raised my arm to wipe my eyes with my sleeve. The deer caught the slight movement, and quickly evaporated into the bright haze.

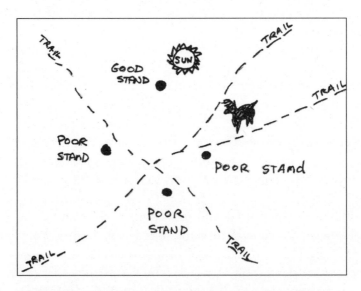

When picking a specific spot for a stand, the prevailing wind direction is the first consideration. Next in importance is ensuring that the sun is on your back or to one side, so you aren't looking into bright light.

The lesson learned from this experience is that, aside from the difficulty of looking directly into the sun without discomfort, when bright sunlight is shining in your direction it tends to magnify even the smallest of movements.

So why not turn this situation entirely around, and make it work the same way against the deer? In other words, if you're an early-morning hunter, you'll want your stand to be situated so that the rising sun is on your back and its bright rays are slanting in the direction where deer are most likely to approach from. If you're an evening hunter, you'll want your back to the West, to achieve the same end. If you hunt both mornings and evenings, you'll probably need two stands in entirely different locations. Sometimes, of course, you might strike it lucky and find a tree where you can compromise by having the sun slightly to your left or right.

With this matter attended to, any deer that approach will have difficulty seeing you because looking in your general direction will mean staring directly into glaring bright light.

PICK THE RIGHT TREE

It's possible to situate a stand so that the sun is not in your eyes, yet you're still bathed in bright light as a result of being too close to perimeter cover edges. It's better to be farther back in the cover, where long tentacles of shadows will help to break up your outline. Some hunters like to have a jumbled maze of heavy brush, vegetation, or tree branches immediately behind them. This is certainly better than being out in the open, but it's more effective to be at least partly encircled by cover.

Many accomplished hunters—bowhunters, in particular—study specific tree species that may best suit their needs. Keep in mind that early in the season, when autumn foliage is still present to obliterate your man-form, virtually any type of tree possessing adequate leafy branches may suffice. The trick is to anticipate what that same tree will look like in weeks to come. After the leaf drop, many tree species become so denuded that not even a sparrow would be concealed from view.

One dramatic exception are the various evergreen species (pines, firs, spruces, cedars), which retain their bushy boughs year-round to afford excellent concealment.

I also like oak trees. Even though an oak's leaves will eventually turn brown and die, they remain securely affixed to their stem attachments long into the dead of winter. The same is true of yellow and tulip poplar, beech, and certain hickory species.

It also pays to select a tree that is not straight-trunked and standing alone like a sentinel, but one which is disfigured, has many gnarled and twisting branches at the intended stand level, and is situated in close proximity to other, similar trees.

Still another important feature I like to see incorporated into both bow and gun stands is moderately thick ground-story vegetation, brush, tag alders, and other growth along the trails leading into my sphere of coverage. The cover should be dense enough so that I have to visually strain to see through it; vegetation this thick hides my presence to any approaching deer, and gives me just the right amount of time to prepare for a shot.

In other words, if I see a buck threading his way in my direction through dense cover, I can rise from a sitting to standing position if necessary, reposition my feet, and raise my bow or rifle. Then, when the deer is about to step into full view, I can begin drawing my bow or bringing the rifle's scope to my eye, all of this done in s-l-o-w motion. Then, when the deer finally steps out of the trailside screening cover and into a shooting alley, no additional movement is necessary on my part. All I have to do is squeeze the trigger or relax my fingertips to smoothly and cleanly release the arrow.

Try engineering your stands in this manner and you'll quickly join ranks with those who believe there simply is no better way to consistently make accurate shots at completely unsuspecting animals.

STAND CAMO THAT WORKS

Nowadays, it seems that everything comes in a box with words on the outside stating "partial assembly required." This is true with most tree stands, as well; if hunters want to be truly inconspicuous, however, they must implement additional measures to hide their stands.

Unfortunately, many hunters do not heed this advice, and each year can be seen trudging into the woods carrying recently assembled portable stands with bright, unpainted wooden and aluminum frame parts that deer are certain to detect, and avoid.

Pick a tree for your stand that is surrounded by other trees with leafy branches. The branches, and the shadows they cast, will help you blend with your surroundings.

After the leaf-drop is complete, relocate your stand to a tree that has many forked trunks and gnarled branches to help absorb your body form.

After many years of hunting experience, I've learned that a properly hidden bow or gun hunter must be virtually absorbed by his surroundings. Serious deer hunters should do everything possible to ensure that their stands melt into the forest's woodwork, so that a wary buck slipping into the vicinity doesn't have a clue that a hunter is in the area.

The first order of business is to hang the stand in your backyard and spray all exposed surfaces with flat black paint. Then, after it dries, use light green or olive drab paint to create vertical bars and stripes to further break up the stand's appearance.

HOW HIGH IS THE STAND?

Many veteran hunters aren't climbing as high as they did in previous years. They've discovered that the only time a high stand is advantageous is when they're in a tree that does not have assorted limbs and leafy branches to break up their outline, or when they're hunting on a steep mountainside and the deer are expected to be coming from an uphill direction. Then and only then is it necessary to be twenty-five or even thirty feet off the ground to be out of a deer's line of vision.

Keep in mind, when bowhunting, that the acute downward angle of the shot increases proportionately with a tree stand's height. In many instances, a portable stand hung no more than ten feet off the ground may be perfectly acceptable if the tree in question has many gnarled, disfigured limbs and leafy branches at that level to adequately conceal the hunter.

If you find an ideal tree but there is little cover at the desirable level, consider gathering some branches, brush, and other cover and attaching it to your stand. Avoid cutting cover from the area immediately surrounding your stand, so you don't eliminate the screens that are needed to block an approaching deer's line of vision.

Since bow and gun hunters both require shooting alleys in several different directions, gather the cuttings from this work and use them.

I like to use a lightweight folding saw for pruning out shooting alleys. Depending upon the location of branches in my chosen tree, I reduce my shooting alley cuttings to straight sapling sections and leafy crown sections. The straight sapling sections can be horizontally tied to my stand, while the leafy crown sections can be inverted and hung upside-down by branch crotches from the horizontals. In just a few minutes, I can make my stand almost completely melt into its surroundings.

GROUND BLIND MASTERY

Few veteran hunters are locked into the mind–set that tree stand hunting is essential to success. Sometimes a savvy hunter will come to the conclusion that he doesn't need a tree stand at all, and that a ground blind is what's really called for.

In fact, one or two ground blinds can save the day when high wind, driving sleet, and plummeting air temperatures make climbing into a tree stand foolhardy.

Unfortunately, many hunters make the mistake of simply tacking a length of camo cloth between two saplings, or piling up brush, and then attempting to merely hide behind the screen of cover. This may suffice for the rifleman who is watching a trail crossing or feeding area 100 yards away. But if a buck slips in close from an unexpected direction, the makeshift blind may cause the hunter to blow his only shooting opportunity. Similarly, such haphazard attempts at blind construction rarely benefit the bowhunter.

A ground blind can save the day when there is no suitable tree for a stand in a hotspot hunting area, or when windy or inclement weather makes climbing trees dangerous.

Two culprits are at work here. First, when attempting to use such a ground blind, the hunter inevitably finds it necessary to peer over the top edge of the blind to watch for deer traffic, thus exposing his head and shoulders to view. Then, when the moment of truth arrives, the nature of his equipment requires him to rise still higher to draw his bow or shoulder his firearm, which not only exposes still more of his upper body torso but also interjects undesirable movements into the hunting equation. Consequently, cover placed behind and around you is just as important, maybe even more so, than cover placed in front of you. The reason is because thick screening cover entirely surrounding your position completely hides your presence from all directions and mutes any subtle movements that you may have to make to bring your equipment into use.

I sometimes even think that the diehard treestand hunter is at a disadvantage. Upon locating favorable sign or a high traffic area for seeing deer activity, the tree-stand hunter must next engineer an appropriate set-up within acceptable shooting range in accordance with his choice of equipment, and this entails a myriad of considerations. Yet, as it so often happens, there simply is no tree of suitable size for enacting an elevated hunting strategy. So the hunter invariably forgets about the sign he has found, no matter how encouraging it may be, and continues his search elsewhere in the hopes of finding both sign and a suitable tree for establishing his waiting location.

Conversely, the ground-blind hunter isn't short-changed in this manner. He doesn't need a tree! He can capitalize upon his discovery by simply designing a hiding place right there, even squarely in the open, knowing in advance that deer will very shortly become accustomed to it and no longer register suspicion or alarm over its presence.

This isn't to say that a ground blind can be carelessly situated. As with a tree stand, wind direction is of unquestionable importance because the hunter will want to ensure that his scent is carried away from the area where he expects deer to appear. Also, the hunter will want to build his blinds in locations designed to place the early-morning and late-afternoon angle of the sun in his favor.

BUILDING YOUR BLIND

Like tree stands, no two ground-blinds ever look alike, but a few construction tips will go a long way toward ensuring the hunter remains as inconspicuous as possible.

An unobtrusive blind is one that closely matches the height of surrounding native cover in the immediate vicinity. If the ground cover is low and sparse, it may be necessary to dig a shallow pit to accommodate a hunter sitting on a stool inside. In the case of gun hunters, the pit can be circular in shape, but bowhunters require a diamond-shaped pit to enable them to draw their bows in frontal, right, and left directions.

If possible, I like to gather native brush and branches and build an igloo-like structure, using twine to hold the cover in place where necessary. I then use pruning shears to cut three small openings to shoot through; these can be round, ten-inch diameter holes for gun hunting, and six- by twenty-inch-tall vertical "slots" for bowhunting.

Another option is poking a number of upright sticks into the ground to encircle the blind site, and then stapling camo cloth in place; be sure to obtain a brand that is rot and mildew proof, to withstand many years of use. Place assorted leafy branches or other native cover around the perimeter of the structure to further break up its appearance.

There are also various types of portable blinds on the market. These are fully-enclosed affairs that pop up quickly with interior wands, and have zippered shooting windows. They look conspicuous, but when left in place all season, in locations where they won't be bothered by other hunters, deer eventually pay them little mind.

Finally, with regards to both tree stands and ground blinds, a partner can be invaluable in fine-tuning your hunting site. Have him walk around your stand or blind and study it from different angles in order to suggest areas that need attention. In the case of a tree stand, perhaps just one leafier branch strategically tied here or there may significantly improve the setup. If it's a ground blind, have your partner face your shooting openings as a nearby deer might periodically do, to ensure your human silhouette is not back-lighted and making you readily visible; in this situation, you need more cover behind you.

In conclusion, remember that although you may know what hypothetically constitutes an ideal tree stand or ground blind for either bow or gun hunting, there's little to be gained by becoming so obsessed with the word "perfect" that anything less is discouraging and reduces your confidence.

Deer hunting is unpredictable, and in the natural world nothing is ever as precise and exact as we might wish it to be. In fact, many of the deer I've taken over the years have been from tree stands or ground blinds where, given the supreme power, I would have placed a bush here or there, altered the growth of a particular branch one inch to the right or left, or done something else to fractionally change the picture. Yet in the final analysis I still enjoyed success.

Chapter 12

Deer Vision

Picture a dark night on a battlefield, deep within enemy territory. You're on patrol, depending upon the combination of darkness and full camouflage to avoid detection. Suddenly, a sniper's rifle cracks in the distance and dust kicks up at your feet! You dive for cover, thanking your lucky stars he was a lousy shot. How did he even see you in the first place?

Undoubtedly, what happened was that you were detected by a starlight scope, through which the sniper saw your brightly illuminated human form as a result of the ultra-violet (UV) pigments in your camo clothing. Although UV is invisible to the naked eye, it glows when seen through the unique optics of a starlight scope. Add to this the fact that you were moving, and you might as well have been a sitting duck in broad daylight.

The above scenario might have taken place years ago, but there's no chance of that now. Military researchers have devised ways to protect our camo-clad troops from the effectiveness of starlight scopes and night-vision binoculars by altering the way combat clothing is made.

By way of background, for many decades virtually all fabric manufacturers put ultra-violet pigments in their dyes so the colors in question appeared bold, bright, and pleasing to the eye.

Similarly, detergent manufacturers to this day continue to add optical brighteners to their soap products. These chemicals leave a ultra-violet reflective residue on the fabric to enhance the original UV color brightness dyes, which tend to fade and dull after repeated washings.

Unfortunately, these ultra-violet brighteners were exactly the thing upon which the effectiveness of UV-sensitive starlight scopes were based. Consequently, it was necessary for government researchers to ban ultra-violet pigments in the dyes commonly used in all fabrics intended for the military. Trouble is, for many years everything was put in the classified information category. Even the soldiers were probably not aware that their military garments were somehow different from conventional street clothing. Thus, the research findings never filtered down to the garment industry that manufactures conventional clothing for the public. This, of course, includes clothing purchased by hunters.

The link between this background information and hunting is that biologists have recently discovered that animals such as deer have the visual apparatus that enables them to detect wavelengths of light deep into the blue end of the color spectrum, where ultra-violet light stands out boldly.

In fact, it has been estimated that a white-tailed deer's sensitivity to ultra-violet color is at least 100 times more acute than that of humans. This means that at all times of day, but particularly during the low-light hours of dawn and dusk and after full dark, deer can see all components of their environment in the same manner an enemy sniper formerly had in using starlight optics.

Consequently, we now know why hunters have experienced the frustration of having deer look squarely in their direction, apparently see something they don't like, and then about-face and disappear, despite the fact that the hunter may have been motionless and wearing full camouflage.

HOW DEER SEE

Of course, it's no longer a secret that deer can distinguish a wide range of colors, but this hasn't always been the case. For generations, hunters were of the opinion that deer perceived their environments in black, white, and shades of gray. However, since no hunter could really prove or disprove what deer actually saw, the myths about black and white vision persisted and were duly passed down from fathers to sons and from magazine editors to trusting readers.

Scientists have conclusively proven that deer can see a wide range of colors. They also can see ultra-violet light, which humans cannot.

Then, in 1977, at the U.S. Department of Agriculture's Veterinary Laboratory in College Station, Texas, a team of biologists decided to use electron microscopes to examine the eyes of live, anesthetized deer.

They immediately detected the presence of a large number of nerve endings, called "rods," in the deers' eyes, but this didn't really come as any surprise. Rods are light receptors and are plentiful in animal species that commonly engage in nocturnal activities. Rods also are motion receptors.

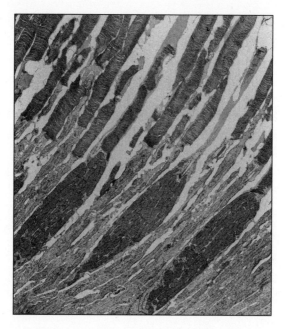

Texas researchers were the first to discover color–receptive cones in the eyes of deer. This electron-microscope photo shows the cones as the dark oval shapes.

Therefore, it's understandable that deer should have a large number of rods to enable them to easily feed and move around in low–light conditions, and that in both darkness and daylight they should be adept at picking up the slightest movements that might forewarn them of a predator on the prowl.

By comparison, humans don't have a high percentage of rods in their eyes. This explains why we possess poor night vision and why, even in broad daylight, slight movements around the periphery of our visual range often go unnoticed.

Next, however, the Texas biologists were shocked to discover a relatively high number of cones in the deer's eyes. Since cones are color receptors, and since humans have an abundance of them and therefore can distinguish even subtle shades of the same hue, it stood to reason that deer might also have color vision capabilities.

The biologists decided to find out by stimulating the eyes of the anesthetized deer with flashes of light spanning the entire range of the color spectrum; the deer's cones responded to those lights in a manner almost identical to the way cones in human eyes involuntarily react. All of this provided the basic proof that deer do indeed possess the anatomical equipment (cones) for discerning colors and that it is indeed functional.

Seven years later, in 1985, a cooperative study of deer vision was undertaken by biologists at Michigan State University and the Michigan Department of Natural Resources.

While the Texas study had confirmed the presence of color vision anatomy in deer, and the functioning of that anatomy under laboratory conditions, the Michigan biologists wanted to test the operation of that color vision under natural conditions with deer fully awake, on their feet, engaging in routine activities.

They did this with penned deer, using standard operant conditioning techniques which entailed the offering of food rewards when the deer

Michigan biologists used food rewards to test deer color vision. Whitetails were found to make correct choices 95 percent of the time.

made correct responses to certain colors and by not rewarding them when their responses were incorrect. As it happened, the deer had no trouble distinguishing between both long-wavelength and short-wavelength colors extending from one end of the color spectrum to the other. In fact—and this is startling—correct responses to the many different colors occurred 95 percent of the time!

THE ULTRA-VIOLET CONNECTION

It was several years after the Michigan researchers confirmed the findings of the Texas biologists that my friend and hunting partner Kurt von Besser began looking into the matter of color vision.

Von Besser is the CEO of ATSKO, the South Carolina-based company that makes products for preserving footwear and garments used by outdoorsmen. He is also a world-class hunter and serious student of wildlife biology who began questioning several intriguing experiences he had had while hunting.

"I began to appreciate the superior vision of animals in pitch darkness several years ago on a horseback hunt in Wyoming," von Besser explains. "Camp was several hours away and we had some steep and hairy terrain to cover in order to reach it. Frankly, I was scared the horse would trip and we'd both fall off the narrow trail down into a deep canyon bottom. So I proceeded to walk, leading the horse, making slow but I thought much safer progress."

Finally, von Besser's guide came back and explained that he should trust his horse because it could see the trail perfectly well and that he'd be safer riding than walking.

"Well, I remounted and, trusting my soul to God and my rear end to the horse, we proceeded," von Besser described. "After a while, I found myself relaxing and trusting the horse more and more. In an area of blowndown timber which we had traversed earlier that morning, where the trail twisted and turned and the horse had to step over countless fallen logs and avoid many branches and uprooted trees, he never even stumbled during the return trip after full dark. I could not even see the horse's head, but he had no problem. This was a question I wrestled with for a long time."

Since von Besser was already familiar with the previous deer color vision studies I mentioned earlier, he began questioning how deer might perceive UV light. Knowing that Dr. Jay Neitz, a vision scientist at the Medical College of Wisconsin, was involved in color-vision research, von Besser sought his help in filling in missing pieces of this growing jigsaw puzzle.

The project proved too enormous in scope for Neitz to undertake alone, so von Besser donated a research grant for Neitz to work at the University of Georgia's School of Natural Resources as part of a cooperative effort. The team included Neitz; famous deer biologists Dr. Larry Marchington and Dr. Karl Miller from the University of Georgia; Dr. Gerald Jacobs and his assistant Jess Deegan, who are animal vision specialists from the University of California at Santa Barbara; and Dr. Brian Murphy, who heads the national Quality Deer Management Association.

What came out of this research shocked hunters nationwide, and has resulted in several new products on the market, not to mention a revolution in the way manufacturers of hunting clothing are now making their garments.

According to the scientists, who presented their findings at a worldwide symposium of big-game biologists, as daylight fades, all creatures, including man and deer, depend more upon the rods in their eyes than their cones. And deer, which often engage in nocturnal activities, have a far greater percentage of rods than humans.

"The significance of this," Miller said at the conference, "is that while cones are more responsive to long wavelength colors at the red end of the color spectrum, rods are more responsive to the short-wavelength blue end of the spectrum."

More specifically, when it comes to cones and color vision, humans have trichromatic physiology, meaning we can see all three of the major colors (red, green, and blue) that span the entire color spectrum and, when blended in various proportions, give us the ability to discern all colors of the rainbow.

Deer, however, have dichromatic physiology, meaning they can see only two of the three major colors (green and blue). And since the peak visual sensitivity of deer is at the blue-yellow point of the color spectrum, after which it abruptly tapers off, deer do not have the sensitivity to see red; it appears to them as a yellowish-brown.

Since a whitetail's visual apparatus peaks at a point in the color spectrum well before a human's visual apparatus, this means its sensitivity level at the blue end of the color spectrum is far more acute than that of humans.

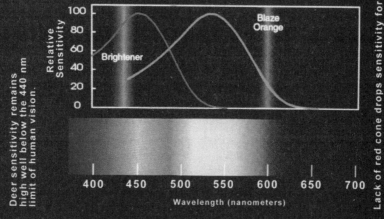

Human and deer vision differ greatly, which is why you should consider using a UV blocking agent.

If you've already guessed that ultra-violet light is found at this farthest, short-wavelength end of the spectrum, you're right! Therefore, what this means is that UV is the one color deer see best of all under all periods of illumination but especially during low light levels and after dark.

Does this mean deer cannot perceive fluorescent orange, which is near the red end of the color spectrum? All research findings suggest they can indeed see it, but not in the same way humans perceive safety orange; deer perceive it as a dull yellow.

More important, keep in mind, as mentioned earlier, that until just recently all fabric dyes (including fluorescent orange) were loaded with UV chemicals — and that hunters have been further enhancing this UV brightness by washing their clothes in detergents to which still more UV chemicals are added!

WHY YOU CAN'T SEE ULTRA-VIOLET

Given all of the above, an obvious question is why can deer see ultra-violet light better than all other hues, and yet we humans cannot?

One reason is because the eyes of deer are larger than those of humans, and their pupils therefore are able to open a larger percentage of their eyes to the available light. Meanwhile, their larger numbers of rods are consequently receiving and being activated by that UV light. Evidence that this occurs can be seen when a vehicle's headlights shine on a deer's eyes after dark, in which case their eyes glow bluish-green due to an anatomical feature called a tapetum at the rear of the deer's eye.

Human eyes do not shine because light passes the retina once, and is absorbed at the back of the eye and lost forever. Conversely, the deer's tapetum recycles the UV light back through the eye to reactivate the photoreceptors again and again, and it's this reflection we see in the headlights.

But even more crucial to UV vision, according to Dr. Neitz, is that humans possess yellow filters in the lenses of our eyes, which are believed to serve two purposes.

First, if we didn't have these anatomical devices to filter out UV light, images interpreted by our retinas would become slightly fuzzed and thereby limit our ability to see fine detail. This is why expert marksmen know their visual acuity can be improved by wearing yellow shooting glasses that block still more short wavelengths of light than the human lens alone is capable of blocking.

"Equally important," Dr. Neitz explains, "the yellow lenses in our eyes, in blocking out UV light, protect our retinas from damage in the same way that sunscreen lotion protects our skin from being burned. Why don't animals such as deer also have yellow filters to protect their eyes from retinal damage? The answer, we believe, is because this retinal damage appears to progress very slowly over decades of life, so protection from UV is less important to animals with much shorter life spans than humans. Also, deer and many other creatures depend upon their ability to detect ultra-violet light to forewarn them of impending danger!"

THE CLOTHING YOU WEAR

The bottom line in all of this is that, unbeknownst to sportsmen, their hunting clothing and especially their camouflage garments have been letting them down by not permitting them to truly blend with their environments. Now you know why it's common to be perched high in a tree stand, totally motionless, the wind in your favor, and yet a deer loping through the immediate area will suddenly slam to a halt, look up squarely in your direction, and then vamoose!

Sure, millions of deer have been killed by hunters, but many other factors have likely contributed to their success by overriding the UV influence. Just one example might be the hunter whose stand is situated in such a manner that most of his body form (and UV-saturated garments) are hidden behind a tree trunk. Consequently, his glowing garments are partially or completely blocked from view of the approaching deer until such time as the animal turns his head and the hunter is able to execute his shot.

In any event, many of the major manufacturers of hunting clothing and accessory gear have begun coming to the forefront by instituting major changes that all hunters should be aware of.

For example, nearly all of the leading manufacturers of camo clothing are now requiring that the fabric mills which produce their bolts of camo cloth no longer add ultra-violet pigments to their dyes. They are also placing "hang-tags" on their garments, informing hunters about UV brighteners and assuring the potential buyer that the garment they have in their hands contains no UV reflective dyes.

If you go into a sporting-goods store and see a camo jacket or pair of coveralls that does not possess such a hang-tag, you can assume one of two things: The manufacturer of that particular brand of clothing has not kept up to date with current research and is still allowing UV dyes in his fabrics; or, he has since discontinued the use of UV dyes in his fabrics but the specific article of clothing in your hands has been sitting in the store a couple of years, in which case you might consider shopping elsewhere.

BIRTH OF U-V-KILLER

Let's say your present selection of hunting garments, which you may have purchased years ago and which therefore may contain UV pigments, still is in excellent condition, and you don't want to throw them away and purchase new clothing. The solution is simple.

When the team of biologists working at the University of Georgia concluded its research, Kurt von Besser immediately launched upon the development of a product he dubbed U-V-Killer, which is specifically designed to block UV radiation emitted by fabric dyes. U-V-Killer literally kills the shocking blue-white glow that is so easily spotted by deer, and thereby allows your chosen garments, especially those imprinted with camo patterns, to blend with the natural cover of your surroundings.

Simply place your hunting clothing (camo or otherwise) on hangers and spray them with U-V-Killer. It dries completely scent-free within twenty-four hours and will withstand six washings.

Since there are always skeptics who tend to scoff at such things, perform this easy experiment. Some evening, take an untreated article of camo clothing to a miniature golf course or anywhere else where bug lights are turned on after dark. Hold the clothing close to one of the lights and notice how it reveals a bright bluish-white glow. Then treat part of the clothing, such as a sleeve, with U-V-Killer and note the dramatic change. This is not magic; it's technically simple. You are covering the reflective dye with a blocking dye, and if you have access to a bug light you can watch this happen right before your eyes.

Be aware that you won't completely benefit from this research if you treat only some of your camo garments. Everything you are wearing must be treated with U-V-Killer. This includes hat, gloves, and face mask. Otherwise, just one brightly glowing item may give you away.

The same applies to safety orange garments that most states require during the firearm seasons; blocking the UV in the fluorescent orange color will render you less visible to deer, especially at dawn and dusk, but not to other hunters.

"In recent years, countless hunters nationwide, who for the first time eliminated the UV reflective glow their clothing was emitting, have been claiming they're seeing far more deer than in previous seasons," Kurt von Besser recently told me. "And they're experiencing far fewer instances in which deer are detecting their movements in raising their bows and firearms."

Another revolutionary product from ATSKO is Sport-Wash, a scent-free laundry detergent that contains no optical brighteners and therefore leaves no UV reflective residue on a hunter's garments. This is the detergent to use when a deer hunter needs to periodically launder clothing previously treated with U-V-Killer, to ensure the clothing never again glows with UV radiation.

Biologists are continually uncovering new insights regarding how deer perceive their environments. The most successful hunters are those who keep up to date with such findings and incorporate them into their hunting strategies.

Chapter 13

Weatherproof Your Hunting Strategy

Deer-hunting days are a lot like poker hands. Sometimes the right thing to do is raise the bet, but other times the smart move is to throw in the towel and hope for a better deal next time around.

We all know diehard card players who refuse to ever pass a hand, and quite often they approach deer hunting the same way. But the most accomplished hunters—those who seem to attach their tags to big bucks every year—know how to pick those particular days to be afield when they're most likely to see action.

Savvy hunters also know how to recognize conditions that shut down deer activity. When this is the case, rather than doggedly remain on stand and predictably see nothing, they spend the off-time scouting a new region, practice shooting on the target range, or perhaps even stacking up brownie points with their boss or family. Then, when Mother Nature deals them a sure winner, they raise the bet by remaining afield until it's too dark.

With the exception of the rut, the weather is the most important factor governing deer activity. Sudden changes in wind velocity, barometric pressure, temperature, and precipitation can either increase or sharply decrease their activity level.

Monitoring changes in barometric pressure and learning to identify cloud formations scudding overhead are two of the most reliable ways of predicting the peaks and valleys of deer activity.

Every serious hunter should have a small weather radio. Some very good ones are no larger in size than a coffee mug and cost less than $30, and since they're battery operated you can take them to deer camp. These radios are tuned to only one channel, that of the National Weather Service, and forecasts for your specific region, no matter where you happen to be at the time, are updated every five minutes.

Illinois biologist Keith Thomas, who has researched the effects of barometric pressure on deer, advises hunters that deer feeding activity is highest at a barometer reading of 29.80 to 30.29. When the barometer is within this range, you should be on stand overlooking a favored food source, near a travel corridor, or in the vicinity of scrapes.

Conversely, if the barometric pressure drops below 29.75, signaling the approach of a storm system, hunters can expect deer to retreat into protected thickets and other heavy-cover bedding areas. Now, stand hunting in the usual areas of deer activity is a wasted effort. If you must play this hand, still-hunt the bedding areas; the driving rain, sleet, and wind will mute your footfalls and make your movements less conspicuous, hopefully allowing you to put deer on their feet for short-range shots.

As the frontal system blows through and the barometer once again rises above 29.80, deer will resume traveling to feeding grounds and engaging in other activities.

CLOUDS TELL ALL

Being a sky-watcher can likewise inform a hunter of impending weather conditions even before a barometric change becomes evident. For example, when altocumulus clouds are gathering on the north or northwest horizon, and winds are coming from the south or southwest, the barometric pressure is about to fall due to a rapidly approaching frontal system. Pack a lunch, hunt pre-scouted feeding areas, and don't even think about returning to camp until dark.

You'll have no trouble recognizing the actual arrival of the frontal system. The puffy, gray altocumulus clouds you were observing will have grown steadily darker. Or, they will have been quickly pushed through your region and been replaced by altostratus clouds, which give the sky a solid, gun-metal gray overcast. The wind velocity, still coming from a southerly direction, will have increased dramatically, and may or may not be accompanied by spits of rain or sleet. That doesn't make any difference, because the high wind itself will have curtailed all deer activity.

Within a day or two, the frontal system will either begin dissipating or will have continued its sweep cross-country. Once again, the heavens tell the story. A clear, starlit night accompanied by a gentle breeze from the north or northwest should tell you to hit the sack early because tomorrow will be splendid for all-day hunting. When you awaken in the morning, you'll undoubtedly notice very high and scattered cumulus clouds, which look like puffy globs of cotton. These conditions indicate the approach of a high-pressure system, moderating conditions, and fair weather. But if they are absent, and there is a halo or corona around the moon, expect still

With the approach of a storm system, deer retreat into
protected thickets and other bedding areas with heavy cover.

another low-pressure frontal system. The halo is the result of moonlight shining through cirrostratus clouds, which are the forerunners of still more unsettled weather destined to arrive within twenty-four hours.

Similarly, if the sky remains a solid leaden gray, with swiftly moving nimbostratus clouds, and the wind continues to emanate from some southerly direction, be prepared for several more days of foul weather.

Lower cirrus clouds—known as mare's tails—also foretell of bad weather, usually in the form of snow. Yet cumulonimbus clouds, with a base several miles wide and an anvil-shaped top that can reach 55,000 feet in height, foretell severe thunderstorms.

All of these cloud formations are depicted in any encyclopedia; also consider buying a small paperback about weather to keep in camp for handy reference.

Finally, always note the color of the evening sky. If the sky at sunset is yellow, be prepared for strong winds the following day, especially during midday. Therefore, stand hunting will be best during the first hours of morning light and the final hours just before dark; if you insist on hunting during midday, the only action you'll likely see will be in the form of still-hunting thick bedding cover or making drives.

Conversely, if the evening sky is red, the following day should be calm and sunny and deer should be intermittently active from dawn to dusk.

IN THE WET

Relative humidity is another weather-related element that also influences deer behavior. In particular, many veteran hunters claim the "dew point" foretells successful or unsuccessful days afield. This phenomenon occurs when the air holds as much moisture as possible at a certain temperature and barometric pressure. At saturation, the temperature and dew point are the same and tend to inhibit deer activity.

Naturally, the amount of humidity varies according to the temperature and location; in the arid Southwest, for example, the air only rarely becomes fully saturated with vapor unless it is raining or snowing. Elsewhere, the general rule to keep in mind is that when the humidity is below 60 percent, deer activity escalates; when it begins rising above 60 percent, deer activity begins to deteriorate.

YOU CAN'T BEAT THE WIND

Obviously, no one can control the wind. But if you understand which types of wind currents make deer feel ill at ease and cause them to go into hiding, versus other winds that may actually pacify them and allow them to engage in their normal routines, you'll know when to stay home and when to grab your gun or bow and head for the hunting grounds.

Frankly, wind direction has never been of much concern to me, except when I consider it in conjunction with cloud formations and changing barometric pressures to forecast what the immediate future holds. Otherwise, since I usually prepare at least five stand locations, it's a simple matter to evaluate the prevailing wind direction and then select whichever stand gives me the greatest advantage.

Of course, after an hour or two on stand, the wind direction may shift; and if you don't relocate to another stand, approaching deer will now readily detect your presence. This is critically important. No matter how much big-buck sign is evident in the area, hunt each of your stands only when conditions are perfect; if temptation gets the best of you and you hunt a hot stand when the wind is wrong, you'll simply destroy it.

Deer react negatively to wind velocity in excess of twelve miles per hour. The strong wind impairs the use of their senses and causes them to cling to thick bedding cover. Now's the time to climb down from your stand, gather your partners, and stage drives.

Wind velocity is just as important as wind direction. Contrary to what many hunters believe, too little wind is just as bad as too much. If the air currents are moving in excess of ten or twelve miles per hour, deer won't move that much. Conversely, if the air is dead calm, deer are likely to be moving, yet they'll be far more easily alerted by even the slightest body movements on your part. Even a barely audible sound such as whisker stubble grating on your jacket collar may send them hightailing for the boondocks.

Consequently, I like for there to be at least a slight amount of wind. A gentle breeze of five miles per hour is perfect. This causes vegetation to sway, and dry leaves to barely rustle, both of which help to camouflage any sounds or movements I may make. Such soft winds are not at all unsettling to deer.

The temperament of the wind is important, too. If the windspeed is erratic, in that relatively calm periods are suddenly disrupted by significant gusts, deer may or may not be on their feet, depending upon the intensity of the gusts. Either way, they will be uneasy and skittish.

The circumstances in which you definitely want to stay home or in camp is when the wind is swirling and eddying in inconsistent directions. These kinds of winds drive me nuts because they seem to buffet you from all directions at once. Or, you'll begin still-hunting with the wind in your face, and only fifteen minutes later the wind direction does a 180-degree about-face. Just about the time you change direction, the wind direction changes still again, until finally you don't know where you're going or what you're doing. Count on one thing, though: your scent is going everywhere at once, and that's a sure ticket to hunting failure.

The best deer-hunting days see the presence of so-called prevailing winds. This means the wind velocity and direction is steady and consistently traveling one way or another. Under these conditions, you can begin enacting an orderly still-hunting effort, or you can situate yourself on a stand with the assurance the wind will not suddenly betray your location.

THE MYSTERY OF THERMALS

A related weather phenomenon—thermal air currents—are more localized in nature. They travel up and down rather than horizontally, and are caused by changes in the air temperature.

In hilly country, and under stable weather conditions, thermal air currents drift downhill, beginning in the late evening and lasting through

early morning. "Downhill" also means down valleys, canyons, creek bottoms, and so on. Then, beginning sometime during the late morning, the
thermals reverse themselves to head back uphill, to the crests of ridges and
to the heads of hollows and draws.

When the topography is relatively flat, thermals drift out of heavy
cover such as forests and move to open places during the evening hours.
This continues until early morning the following day. Then, about mid-
morning, there is a reversal, with the thermals drifting from open places
toward heavy cover.

In all of this, a critical thing to keep in mind is that a prevailing wind
will cancel out any thermal air currents.

With this knowledge, it's easy for a savvy hunter to better his chances
of catching deer unaware. Deer, of course, continually monitor the wind
for any bits of scent that may indicate approaching danger. When there is
no wind, they use thermals to serve as their sentries.

This is one reason why mature bucks living in hilly terrain head for high
ground to spend the midday hours. They do it to have a good view of what's

When there's little or no
wind, deer use thermal air
currents to their advantage.
Unlike wind currents which
travel horizontally, thermals
rise and fall vertically in
accordance with changes
in the air temperature. This
is why bucks bed on high
ground during midday, to
continually monitor what's
going on below them.

going on below, but also because the typical upslope drift of the thermals during the daylight hours will warn them of anything on the prowl. Conversely, most deer spend most of the night and dawn hours in the lower elevations; food and water are not only most plentiful there, but the thermal air currents have now shifted and lower ground is simply the safer place to be.

The same principle applies in flat country. The deer move into heavy cover to spend the late morning and early afternoon hours, partly to hide and rest, but also because the thermals will be in their favor; in the evening and early morning they are able to move into more open areas to feed and drink while still being on the alert.

Hunters can benefit immensely from this. When still-hunting, plan your movements so that thermal air currents are working in your favor, not against you. In hill country, this means hunting upslope in the direction of bedding sites until no later than perhaps 10:00 a.m. Through the late morning, afternoon, and sometimes even into the very early evening, you must be on high ground such as ridges, hillside benches, and canyon rims. In the flatlands, stay deep in the forests and heavy-cover regions during midday, and work the edges and clearings only during the evening or very early in the morning.

THE NEMESIS OF SNOW

Hunters who live in northern states traditionally hope for good tracking snow on opening day. But in reality, snow is advantageous only when it has fallen several days before opening day.

As Dr. Ken Nordberg, a whitetail researcher from Minnesota, explains, "deer become very fearful when snowfall is sudden or significant. Their entire world has suddenly changed, and no longer are there any familiar scents, sounds, or sights to soothe their nervous, paranoid personalities. After a sudden, heavy snow, deer will remain in their beds for at least forty-eight hours, until they have mentally adapted to the change. If you're inclined to pray for favorable weather, don't pray for snow on the eve of opening day!"

Take note that we're referring to a sudden deluge of snow. This is when you want to toast your stocking feet before the fireplace. On the other hand, light snow sifting gently downward, with little or no accumulation, is an excellent time to be afield.

Deer react negatively to sudden, deep snowfall because of the abrupt change in their environment. They may bed for forty-eight hours until they've adapted to the change before resuming normal activities.

Chapter 14

How the Experts Call Deer

A non-hunter undoubtedly would be very surprised to learn that deer use a wide variety of vocalizations to communicate with each other. But serious deer hunters know better. In fact, at a recent trade show for hunters (appropriately called the SHOT show), I counted twenty-seven different booths where manufacturers were displaying their company's selection of deer calls. Several of the companies had ten or more variations of calls in their line-up.

This trend had its birth in the late 1970s when biologists Dr. Thomas Atkeson and Dr. Larry Marchington at the University of Georgia, and Dr. Harry Jacobson of Mississippi State University, released the results of a research project in which they tape-recorded the vocalizations of deer and associated them with specific types of behavior.

Although the biologists identified fifteen different types of sounds emitted by whitetails under varying circumstances, the ones of greatest importance to hunters are: agonistic (sometimes called combative or aggressive) calls, tending grunts, alarm snorts, maternal bleats, contact calls, and wheeze-snorts.

Of all deer vocalizations, the alarm snort is the one most recognized by hunters. A spooked deer produces this noise by violently expelling air through the nostrils with the mouth closed; in most cases it's a reaction to something alien which the deer has smelled but not yet seen or heard. Because a whitetail blatantly declares its own location when it makes such a sound, it is believed the snort is a means of announcing impending danger to other nearby deer that may not be in a windward position to catch the foreign odor themselves.

Upon hearing such snorts, usually made in sequence several seconds apart as the deer is beginning to flee from the area, the hunter should intuitively know that he is the source of the odor and the cause of the alarm. In most instances, this means his stand location was ill-chosen with regards to the prevailing wind direction, or that through sheer happenstance the deer approached from downwind. In either case, when this happens to me I feel that particular area is "blown out." I consequently abandon the stand for another one that's located at least several hundred yards away. I may not return to the blown-out stand for a week or more, and when I do return, if a deer catches me a second time I'll pull the stand for the remainder of the season.

In a cooperative study, biologists at the University of Georgia and Mississippi State University discovered that whitetails make fifteen different types of vocalizations.

Agonistic calls generally consist of two types of grunts. The "low grunt" is emitted by both bucks and does on a year-round basis. It's a close-contact method of communication and represents the lowest level of aggressive interaction when one deer, invariably a subordinate, encroaches just a bit too closely upon the specific spot where a higher-ranking animal is feeding or drinking. When an inferior deer takes this liberty, the higher-ranking animal makes a deep, low-pitched gutteral blat. This usually wards the intruder away; if not, the dominant animal may then lay his ears back, dash forward, and administer a sharp kick with a foreleg hoof. The subordinate deer then knows to keep his distance.

The grunt snort as identified by biologists, but which call manufacturers refer to as the "snort wheeze," is far more of a combative sound. Although both males and females produce the sound, it is more common among posturing males when they are attempting to establish their hierarchal pecking order or when they are squaring off against each other during the mating season. Usually, the sound consists of two to six snorts in rapid succession, just as the deer are lunging at each other. Its purpose is to intimidate the other deer, and reminds me of the loud shout a karate expert uses just prior to delivering a blow with feet or hands.

Maternal bleats are the soft, almost soprano-like mewings produced by fawns and yearlings when they want the attention of their mothers. In most cases the attention they desire is to suckle and be groomed by licking, although this behavior is more typical of the spring and early summer. Later in the year, maternal bleats are usually produced by that year's slightly older offspring that have become separated from their mothers and are uneasy about being alone.

Adult females about to experience estrus frequently make a similar bleat to announce their readiness to any bucks within earshot. It sounds just like the mewing of a fawn, but is louder and deeper. Hunters sitting on stand near scrapes frequently mimic this sound in the hopes of drawing a nearby buck's attention.

Tending grunts are important for hunters to learn to recognize. These are the vocalizations made by sexually excited males in two types of circumstances. A buck returning to a primary scrape and discovering a doe's estrus odor in the air will put his nose tight to the ground like a bird-dog making scent and will walk in a rapid, stiff-legged gait as he tries to catch up with the doe. Or, when the buck is actually in the company of a doe who is not quite ready to be serviced, he will follow closely behind, grunting and licking her hindquarters and often chasing her for brief distances until she eventually agrees to stand.

I once wrote a magazine article in which I said the tending grunt a buck makes in these two circumstances reminds me of a euphoric hog rooting around in a feed bin. Since then I've come to realize that many urban hunters have never heard the sounds that pigs make. To be more accurate, I now say that it sounds precisely like your stomach growling when you're hungry!

MEET THE EXPERTS

As a result of the studies conducted by deer scientists, deer call companies were born and a new industry started to grow. Today, there literally are dozens of manufacturers of deer calls that are far more sophisticated than our ancestors could have ever dreamed of using.

It has been my good fortune to have close friendships with the founders of several of these companies. In particular, I've spent countless hours afield with Harold Knight and David Hale of Knight & Hale Game Calls, Will Primos of Mississippi-based Primos Game Calls, Brad Harris of Missouri-based Lohman Game Calls, and Ron Jolley and Jerry Peterson of Tennessee-based Woods-Wise Game Calls.

The collective knowledge of these individuals alone could occupy an entire book, and so this section is merely a distillation of their advice to hunters who want to master the art of calling deer. Fortunately, this summary shouldn't leave the hunter deficient in his education, because game-call companies often provide cassette tapes or videos with their calls. These describe when, where, and how to use that particular call; the hunter can listen to the experts actually calling, and then practice with the call until he achieves the identical volume, pitch, and cadence.

GRUNT CALLS

It was in 1984 that Brad Harris and his partner, Bill Harper, invented the grunt call. Since then, grunt calls have become far and away the most popular among hunters, and every manufacturer in the business has obliged them with subtle variations of Harris's original creation.

"The great shortcoming among many hunters is blowing into them too loudly and for too long," Harris has observed.

And it's true. Maryland biologist C. J. Winand determined that a grunt vocalization averages only .7 second in duration, while Indiana biologist Morris Wills once told me that unless there is absolutely no wind, a buck grunt can't be heard from more than 200 yards away. My advice? Go with the new calling science and make short, snappy grunts that make you sound like a wimp.

Take what happened one year in Kentucky's Land-Between-the-Lakes region when I attempted to grunt a respectable eight-pointer into shooting range. At first, the deer registered a mild interest by jerking his head upright and cupping his ears in my direction. This stand-off, with

Brad Harris of Lohman Game Calls invented the now-famous
grunt call with the telltale ribbed tube that allows the sound to be
directed away from the hunter's location. Variations of his design
are now marketed by all leading deer-call manufacturers.

the animal about eighty yards away, lasted maybe five minutes. When it
became clear the deer wasn't going to come any closer, I tried to coax him
with a series of bolder, louder challenges.

At that, the deer protruded his tongue laterally out the side of his
mouth, lowered his head, and slinked away. Right then, when the buck
exhibited this universal whitetail fear response, I knew I'd blown it.

"You'll attract more flies with just a little sugar than a lot of vinegar,"
my hunting partner Harold Knight later explained.

"One of the biggest mistakes made by deer hunters is being too aggressive with a grunt call," David Hale added. "That only serves to intimidate
most bucks and scare them away."

Later, back at Harold and David's call-manufacturing facility, I was shown their latest video on calling deer. I was amazed to see what really goes on in the vocal lives of whitetails.

"When attempting to call a wary white-tailed buck, you have to create an aura of confidence that makes him feel comfortable," Knight emphasizes. "Remember, whitetails are very gregarious, social animals. Particularly when they're slowly feeding through cover, and occasionally lose sight of each other, they like to monitor each other's location with short, low-volume contact calls."

"Contact calls can be used any time of year, but they're especially effective on bucks at the very beginning of the season when they're still adhering to their bachelor groupings," Jerry Peterson explains. "Essentially, a buck making a contact call is saying, 'come here, now,' or 'I'm here, where are you?'"

"In all of this, never lose sight of the fact that deer adhere to very rigid pecking orders, and that they respect each other's rank. Peterson continues. "Moreover, keep in mind that in any deer population, the majority of the bucks are subordinates. Only a few—the largest and oldest—achieve dominant status. Therefore, if you grunt too often, too loudly, and too forcefully, the only thing you'll accomplish is scaring most of the male deer."

What Knight and Peterson say makes sense. After all, who wants to intentionally risk a fight with a bully, suffer a bruised ego, and maybe receive battle scars in the process? Yet that is exactly the type of intimidation a buck may feel he's in for if he responds to a call supposedly being made by a superior animal.

"On the other hand," Hale explains, "imagine the weakling on the beach who, by his very presence, invites trouble. That's the kind of illusion you want to create in the deer woods. You want to sound like a wimp deer that is very low on the hierarchal totem pole, so that virtually any other buck in the vicinity will feel confident that he can share your company, and if anything gets out of hand give you a whipping."

BUCKS AND DOES TOGETHER

While a grunt call may draw the interest of a buck almost anytime during fall and winter, there is a specific period just before does begin coming into estrus when bucks are the most vocal. This is the pre-rut, when bucks and does play a cat-and-mouse game in preparation for breeding, during which a buck's desire to mate reaches feverish heights.

Call designer David Hale advises that you don't call too loudly or forcefully, or you'll sound like a bully buck and scare most deer away. Sounding like a wimp buck is more likely to result in a mature buck coming to challenge you.

During the pre-rut and peak rut, combining the use of a grunt call and rattling antlers can produce heart pounding action, especially in the vicinity of scrapes.

The unique thing about all of this, something that many hunters don't fully comprehend, is the exact tonal quality of the buck's grunting. It is not simply a sound produced by the buck exhaling air, but a combination of rapid exhaling and inhaling in staccato-like fashion. Liken the entire thing, if you will, to the tonal irregularity exhibited by a person trying to jog and talk at the same time.

It's this breathless excitation in the buck's grunting that attracts other bucks within earshot, and causes them to rush to the scene in an attempt to horn in on the action.

What Harold Knight and David Hale discovered when video and audio taping deer is that this unique grunting sound cannot be reproduced by simply blowing (exhaling) into a conventional grunt tube. That, in turn, caused them to "re-invent" the grunt call. The result, which is appropriately called The Hyper-Ventilator, allows a hunter to rapidly and alternately inhale and exhale through the same end of the tube in order to produce the exact, breathless tonal quality of a buck just moments before he breeds with a doe. Since this revelation, most other callmakers have come out with their own variations of inhale–exhale grunt calls.

KNOW WHEN TO STOP

"When using a grunt call, keep in mind your own reaction to various sounds," Brad Harris suggests. "If you hear something in the distance but aren't sure what it is, you'll wait for confirmation in the form of more sounds. If no more sounds come, you'll forget the incident.

"Deer are the same way," Harris continues. "If you see a buck turn and look in your direction when you grunt, don't stop! Keep on grunting to hold his attention. At the same time, never lose sight of the fact that whenever you're calling, you're broadcasting news about your specific location. Therefore, as the deer approaches closer and closer, continuing to call increases the chance that the deer will become aware of your human presence. And when that happens, it's all over."

"When using any type of call, if your buck is rapidly closing the distance to your location, put the danged call down!" Jerry Peterson adds. "The call has performed its function, and now you should let him come the rest of the way of his own accord. Make him hunt you! Only if the deer appears to lose interest, turns, and begins moving in another direction should you attempt to softly coax him back."

It's also worth noting that the volume of the calling effort should always be considerably toned down as the deer approaches. Not only will grunting too loudly make it easier for a buck to peg your specific location but, as I mentioned before, it is likely to also have an intimidating effect and cause him to vamoose with his tail tucked between his legs.

BLEATING AND BAWLING

Every serious hunter should carry several calls. His mainstay will undoubt-edly be a grunt tube, yet there are times when a bleat call, which simulates a young deer in distress, will bring in the biggest buck of all. If that sounds like an unlikely situation, consider how this particular vocalization influ-ences whitetails.

In the animal kingdom, which includes domesticated animals as well as wildlife, females which have previously given birth at least once feel an instinctive need to protect the young of their species, even if a given indi-vidual is not their own offspring.

"One time I was sitting in a tree stand. About 250 yards away were a doe with two yearlings, which I am sure were hers," relates Will Primos. "When I bleated with my call, she immediately threw her head up high and became instantly alert as she looked straight in my direction. When I bleated a second time, she left her two offspring and charged straight toward me on a dead run, even though the distress call I was simulating couldn't have been from one of her own young."

Although a bleat call brings in more does than anything else, bucks quite often respond as well. When a mature, dominant buck is taken through the assistance of a bleat call, however, it is not the call, per se, that proves to be his undoing, but rather his libido. The reason, as we've noted, is because once a doe begins climbing to the zenith of her estrus cycle, there is nothing a hunter can do to coax a tending buck away from her side.

Faced with this frustrating situation, most hunters either throw up their hands in despair or continue to futilely blow on their grunt calls.

"There's an easy solution to this," Primos emphasizes. "Simply, if you cannot grunt in a rut-crazed buck, use your bleater to call in the doe, and the buck will follow her right to your location."

It's even becoming a rather standard routine among insightful hunters to restrict their grunting to the pre-rut preparation period. As the peak of the rut nears, they then use only their bleat calls. Even though a doe might be right in the middle of her estrus cycle and is repeatedly being serviced by an amorous buck, she still feels the maternal instinct to come to the assistance of a fawn or yearling that she perceives to be injured or in distress.

If you are sitting in a tree stand or ground blind and there are no deer anywhere in sight, blow on the call about ten times once every twenty minutes. Don't blow any more frequently than this, because on a calm day deer can hear this call up to one-half mile away; even if they respond immediately, it will take them a bit of time to travel the distance.

"If no deer are in sight, blow your bleat call as loud as possible," Knight says. "Don't be afraid to really put on some theatrics, with a lot of intense wailing and feeling. If you've ever heard a live fawn tangled in a fence or being pulled down by a coyote, it screams its lungs out and almost makes your hair stand on end. That's the very type of intensity and volume you want to project with your call."

"On the other hand," Will Primos adds, if you have a deer in sight in the distance, use a slightly reduced volume by cupping your palm over the end of the call and blowing less forcefully; yet do continue to embellish your calling with plenty of soft cries of distress."

Incidentally, two of Primos's innovations for bowhunters are grunt calls and bleat calls that can be held securely in the side of the mouth while drawing a bowstring and releasing an arrow; this idea eliminates the hand movements associated with raising and lowering a call to the mouth and thus possibly alerting a deer that is close to one's stand.

FINE-TUNING YOUR CALLING

From my experience, using a grunt or bleat call is best accomplished in mildly windy weather. True, your call won't carry the same far distance as on a dead calm day, but there are other advantages that fall in your favor.

The noise of the wind itself, and the associated sounds of rustling leaves and clacking tree branches, interferes with a deer's sense of hearing.

Consequently, an approaching deer quite often becomes confused over where the call originated. If it's a buck, it expects to eventually encounter a rival buck doing the grunting, and if it's a doe it expects to find a young deer in distress. When this visual contact doesn't take place, the responding deer begins to wander erratically, apparently presuming the deer it heard is still farther ahead, or off to one side or the other.

In any event, when a responding deer becomes momentarily disoriented by not being able to find and visually identify what its ears have told it is there, it becomes careless and makes mistakes. It's thought processes have not been programmed to expect you lurking overhead in a tree stand or hunkered down in a ground blind. This slight edge in your favor may spell a clear shot at a totally unsuspecting animal.

WHISTLING FOR DEER

"When a running deer hears a shrill whistle, its first inclination is to slam to a halt until such time as it is able to use its ears, eyes, or nose to identify the source of the sound before taking further evasive action. To continue moving, without making this identification, would incur the risk of perchance running right into the lap of danger," explains Brad Harris.

That's why Lohman developed a concept in calls with the Whistlin' Deer Stopper, which is intended for use when a hunter inadvertently spooks a deer out of cover and it begins bounding away, or when a hunter playing the role as a stander during a deer drive has a buck running through his immediate area of coverage.

"The logic behind this call is easy to understand," Harris says. "Conventional whistling with the lips pursed together is an age-old, proven method that is effective in stopping moving deer in their tracks. The pitch is so much higher and uncharacteristic of anything deer customarily hear in the woodlands that it literally overloads them with mental confusion and brings them to a stop to see what the heck is going on. My problem, which is shared by countless other hunters, is that I cannot produce a high-pitched whistle with any degree of volume."

And that is exactly what's needed if the wind is blowing, or the deer is far away, or the animal itself is making plenty of noise crashing away through dry cover. Lohman's Whistlin' Deer Stopper is perfect for any of these situations because both its volume and pitch carry well beyond 100 yards, even under the most adverse conditions.

Chapter 15

Biologists Demystify Antler Rattling

"Okay, kids," as Dave Letterman would say, "it's pop quiz time."

1. Texas hunters are credited with inventing antler-rattling, and it essentially works only in the Lone Star State. True or False?
2. Rattling antlers for big bucks is most effective during the peak of the rut. True or false?
3. You'll see more bucks if you don't rattle too loudly, as this will intimidate deer of all ages. True or false?
4. The size of the rattling antlers and how you hold them and mesh them together is critically important to your success. True or false?

If you answered "true" to any of the above questions, it's time to go back to school.

First and foremost, rattling antlers is definitely not a modern-day hunting innovation, and it did not evolve solely in Texas. Across a broad range of south-central and Midwestern states, Shawnee, Osage, Quapaw, Cado, and Apache Indians were known to "rattle-in" deer hundreds of years ago by simply knocking two dry sticks together. Moreover, since then the technique has been found to be effective across the whitetail's entire range; in short, it works as well in Maine, Ohio, Georgia, Wisconsin, and Idaho as it does in Texas.

For many years, our knowledge pertaining to the technical aspects of rattling (when, how, where) has been fuzzy because deer biologists haven't offered much insight. Historically, they've focused their research on such esoteric subjects as deer nutrition, diseases, and population dynamics. This has left hunters to their own personal field experiences and experimentation, often resulting in nothing more substantive than deer camp speculation.

Recently, however, some of the country's most respected biologists have been taking a close look at techniques such as antler rattling; they're doing so with measurable scientific procedures, and are providing hunters with valuable answers.

I was thinking about that one crisp morning last fall during the pre-rut as I sat on a hillside overlooking a deep ravine. I'd spotted a buck bedded on the opposite slope about 200 yards away. After clashing my rattling antlers together for only fifteen seconds, I watched as he literally exploded out of his bed and charged straight in my direction.

Contrary to what many believe, antler-rattling works anywhere that whitetails live. The size and shape of the antlers have little to do with their effectiveness.

As it happened, the deer never presented an acceptable shot and eventually slinked away, but he nevertheless had positively responded to my effort. The perplexing thing was that just the day before, in early afternoon, I'd seen the same buck bedded in the same place. I rattled from the same exact location, and the deer showed absolutely no interest. Why did he go crazy one time but not the other?

MEET THE DEER DOCTORS

Many of the scientific explanations underpinning antler-rattling success have come from deer biologists Larry Weishuhn and Mickey Hellickson.

Weishuhn, a long-time acquaintance, has penned countless words on whitetail behavior for the leading deer-hunting magazines. And Hellickson, a member of the famous deer-research team at the University of Georgia, spent three years working on a doctoral degree on the subject of antler rattling.

A good deal of Hellickson's research has also involved radio-telemetry studies of deer during the rut with noted researchers Larry Marchington and Charles DeYoung. By previously outfitting live-trapped deer with radio collars, releasing them, and then using receivers to pinpoint their locations, they were able to monitor the daily behavior of the animals. In this particular study, they were able to slip quietly to within 200 yards of each animal and then rattle, knowing full well each deer would be able to hear them.

"Many of the located bucks we rattled to responded a second and third time, just as they did the first," Hellickson said.

But what about the buck that aggressively responded to my antler rattling one day but not the next? This is explained by Hellickson's investigations in a recent control-study. which revealed that, of 111 bucks that responded to antler rattling, eighty-three percent of them responded during the early morning hours of 7:30 a.m. to 10:30 a.m. Far fewer animals responded to antler rattling at noon, and still fewer responded during midday rattling sequences.

So clearly, if you want to stack the odds in your favor, the best time to rattle-in a buck is in the early morning.

WHAT'S THE APPEAL OF RATTLING TO BUCKS?

The sounds of antler rattling are an integral part of the social lives of male deer.

Fighting bucks are a sight to behold, but it should be said that legitimate battles between mature males are actually quite uncommon. A genuine brawl is most likely to occur when a mature buck, for whatever reason, leaves his own breeding territory, where his hierarchal ranking is well-established, and ventures into a different area inhabited by another mature, dominant buck.

The predictable outcome is that both animals become enraged at the other's presence, with quick charges and violent episodes of antler clashing the result. Ultimately, one of the combatants accepts defeat and either slinks away or is chased from the vicinity by the victor.

A passerby cannot mistake the amphitheater where a genuine buck fight has recently taken place. Quite often, as much as twenty-five square yards of sod and forest duff are torn up and urine-dampened, and the air is thick with the pungent aroma of tarsal scent. Several friends who commercially produce deer-hunting videos have told me that in their entire professional careers they've observed genuine buck fights on only a handful of occasions.

As a result, when hunters claim to have observed two bucks fighting, in a majority of cases what they've witnessed is not fighting at all but the far more commonplace occurrence known as sparring.

Sparring among bucks is a mild-mannered effort to climb the hierarchal totem pole, and such interactions don't even begin to resemble a vicious "take no prisoners" encounter. Instead, it consists primarily of posturing, bluffing, and other nonviolent attempts at intimidation. Certainly, there's sure to be some antler meshing between the two animals, but it is generally very toned down in terms of aggressive intent; the bucks merely bring their heads together, engage their racks, push until resistance is felt, twist their necks several times, and then quickly separate. Moments later, they may then register total disinterest in each other and return to feeding only scant yards apart.

This ongoing, periodic shadow-boxing may begin as soon as antler velvet is shed in early fall. It will continue to escalate in intensity as the hormonal flow of testosterone begins reaching its zenith in mature animals, causing them to assume properly assigned hierarchal roles far more seriously. Yet by this time, most mature bucks have long since staked out their individual breeding grounds where they simply do not have much interaction with other mature males; hence, the infrequent occurrence of near-psychotic fighting activities.

This background helps to explain why many insightful hunters enjoy tremendous results rattling in bucks, while other hunters have so little success that many of them even claim that rattling isn't very effective.

"Hunters who aren't having much success are undoubtedly doing their rattling in the wrong location and at the wrong time of year," says Mickey Hellickson. "Also, they probably aren't rattling as loudly as they should."

According to deer biologist Mickey Hellickson, antler-rattling success hinges mostly upon two things: rattling in the right location and at the right time of year.

Hellickson's research involved four different combinations of long, short, loud, and quiet rattling sequences. The biologists didn't detect any difference in response rates based upon the length of the rattling sequences, but they clearly noticed that bucks responded more quickly and more aggressively to the loudest sequences.

"Always make an effort to infuse as much realism as possible into your rattling," advises Weishuhn. "When two bucks are really going at it, they don't just stand there and butt heads. It's like a barroom brawl in which the 'furniture' of their environment is busted up. So stomp the earth with your boots, roll rocks downhill, break branches, and rake the antlers through nearby brittle brush to simulate the real thing."

Don't be bashful about putting on some theatrics. Make your rattling sound like an authentic buck fight by raking the antlers through brush and leaves and by stamping your feet on the ground.

"This is also an ideal opportunity to use calls," Brad Harris of Lohman Calls suggests. "We've even developed what we call a Big Buck Calling Kit, which contains our Triple-Tone Grunt Call and Adult Doe Bleat. With this combination of calls you can alternately produce bold, throaty buck grunts while rattling, and also love-sick doe bleats to simulate the presence of an estrus female as a reward for the outcome of the fight."

GET INTO THE RHYTHM

The actual technique of antler rattling, it seems, has long been cloaked in mystery. But I recently had an experience which demonstrates that it is not at all complicated.

I'd just climbed into my tree stand and was using a haul rope to pull up my bow and rattling antlers. As everything dangled freely in the morning breeze, the antlers lightly clinked against each other and the bow's riser, sounding almost like wind chimes.

Moments later, I heard crashing noises coming through a brushy thicket about seventy-five yards away, and a six-point buck came charging in my direction! Apparently, the deer deciphered the clinking noise as being the sound of two bucks sparring, and that prompted his immediate investigation of his breeding grounds. So there I stood, my gear still dangling ten feet beneath me and the deer quickly homing in upon my location. Needless to say, the buck soon realized he'd been duped, spotted me, swapped ends, and disappeared.

Although I didn't get that buck, I did receive a valuable education that has since reconfirmed itself many times. The lesson learned is that where and when you rattle is far more important than any particular method of holding the antlers or clashing them together; although as noted earlier, the louder your performance the better.

One element—timing—is equally important, because it's necessary to give any buck within earshot ample opportunity to reach your location. From my experience, a good rule of thumb is to rattle continuously for about three minutes, wait for five minutes, go through your routine again for another three minutes, and then wait still another ten minutes. Some bucks rush right in, yet others are late responders. Also, depending upon the wind and weather, the sounds of rattling carry variable distances on a given day, and a deer may have to travel (usually in sneak-mode) several hundred yards to reach your location.

If nothing appears after a multiple rattle-and-wait sequence, move to another area because it's safe to conclude that either no bucks are within earshot of your rattling, or any bucks in the immediate area are simply not interested.

I emphasize this, because when it comes to antler rattling, exposure is the name of the game.

"From radio-telemetry studies, we've learned that bucks may roam as far as eight to ten miles during the rut," Weishuhn explains. "So the more ground you cover and the more places you rattle, the greater the number of bucks that will hear your theatrics, and this translates into more responses and more shots."

I call this philosophy "rattling on the run," and it can mean covering many miles of terrain each day.

THE "WHEN" FACTOR

The University of Georgia deer biologists have concluded that the rutting season is far and away the most productive time to rattle. This may seem obvious, yet keep in mind the rut is divided into three distinct periods: the pre-rut, peak-rut, and post-rut. Most hunters might assume that the peak of the rut is the best time to rattle in a mature buck, because that's when they're in the chase phase, looking for receptive does and therefore not tolerating other males in their respective regions. But surprisingly, the biologists learned that the greatest response to rattling among mature bucks actually occurs during the post-rut!

Equally eye-opening, the second greatest response frequency occurred during the pre-rut, before the majority of does have been successfully bred. The smallest percentage of responses actually occurred during the peak rut.

Another intriguing discovery is this: The researchers learned that the majority of animals rattled in during the peak of the rut invariably were immature bucks. During the pre-rut and post-rut, fewer animals responded to antler rattling, but those that did respond were, by a large percentage, the largest bucks. This leaves hunters with a choice. Assuming your field time is limited due to job and family responsibilities, would you rather devote your rattling time to the peak rut and see lots of immature bucks? Or would you rather concentrate on the pre- or post-rut, see few animals, but have the best chance of calling in a real whopper?

Biologists explain that, during the pre-rut, most mature bucks are pre-occupied with chasing after does that are about to climb to the top of their estrus cycles; they are therefore more likely to respond to the sounds of antler clashing. During the peak rut, mature bucks have solidified their tending bonds with does that are fully in estrus, and are therefore less responsive to rattling than immature bucks, which have so far been repressed from breeding. And during the post-rut, young bucks have resumed their bachelor groupings to search for food, while loner mature bucks are continuing to actively "troll" for those few does that have not yet come into estrus; now, they're again inclined to respond to the sounds of rattling, which simulates two rival bucks battling over a nearby doe-in-waiting.

It's important to emphasize that bowhunters generally enjoy the best rattling action during all three rutting periods, simply because most state's firearm seasons have not yet opened. North of the Mason-Dixon line, the three-stage rutting period usually spans the last two weeks of October and the first three weeks in November; in the deep South, the rutting period is protracted and generally spans the months of December and January, allowing firearm hunters to also get in on the action.

THE "WHERE" FACTOR

Both Weishuhn and Harris tell us that rattling from a high vantage point should be the focus of every hunter's attention. No one knows why, but an oddity of nature is that most animal species that respond to various types of calls are extremely difficult to entice downhill. Elk, turkeys, and especially deer are far more inclined to respond if they are able to either travel uphill or at least remain on the same level of elevation.

Of course, antler rattling can be done either from a tree stand, or while on the ground, with each approach having its own advantages and disadvantages.

Teaming up with a partner increases bowhunting success. If the shooter is out in front, a deer approaching the rattling sound will walk right past him and offer a close, broadside shot.

"Keep in mind that when a buck responds to rattling, you become the hunted," Weishuhn notes. "The buck will be making a diligent attempt to pinpoint the source of the rattling noise, and make visual contact with what he perceives are other bucks encroaching upon his breeding territory."

Moreover, since deer don't live in trees, a responding buck will be riveting his attention upon the ground-level terrain ahead of him. As a result, a hunter perched in a tree stand has a much better chance of going undetected than a hunter rattling on the ground. Also, from an elevated position, it's much easier to look down and through cover to survey your surroundings and spot an approaching deer.

"In one of our studies," says biologist Mickey Hellickson, "we had a hunter on the ground rattling. We also had an observer in a nearby thirty-foot tower watching for bucks, and videotaping those that came in. Of the 111 bucks that responded to the rattling, the hunter on the ground never saw sixty-three of them."

Due to intervening brush and other cover that can obscure one's view on level terrain, a lightweight tree stand with shoulder straps is critical gear for rattling on the run, and thus seeing a majority of that bucks that respond to your effort.

Conversely, those hunters who don't have the energy or inclination to carry a portable stand over several miles of terrain and use it to scurry up and down a dozen or more trees every morning, should keep the term "elevated" in mind. In other words, when hunting level terrain, try to find knolls, knobs, or gentle rises to rattle from that allow you to look down and through surrounding cover.

GETTING IT ALL TOGETHER

Wherever a hunter plans to rattle in the morning, the best location by far is near scrapes. During all three rutting periods, mature bucks will not tolerate other bucks near their scrapes. Since a scrape can be considered a type of "bait" that a buck has set out to attract a doe, he doesn't want another buck breeding any doe that comes to investigate.

But if a hunter plans to rattle during midday, which is far less productive, the best location is not around scrapes, but downwind of a buck's bedding area.

Lastly, another finding by the deer doctors is that the highest number of buck responses to antler rattling take place when wind velocity is lowest. Also, be sure to take advantage of days when there is significant cloud activity, because biologists have recorded far more responses from bucks when there is heavy cloud cover compared to little or no overcast. Unfortunately, until we can teach deer to talk, we may never know why this occurs.

Chapter 16

Stalking and Still-Hunting Skills

An old sage once observed that man learns more from his failures than from his successes. This unquestionably applies to my twenty years worth of trial-and-error learning experiences in attempting to sneak up on white-tailed bucks.

For example, take the apparently simple matter of deciding upon the best time of day to be prowling around in search of a deer. For many years I subscribed to the conventional wisdom of sitting on stand early and late in the day when the animals are moving around naturally, then spending the midday hours still-hunting because that is generally when deer are not moving.

During those years, I took plenty of deer from my tree stands during dawn and dusk hours, yet I rarely got close enough to a buck during mid-day hours to place a telling shot. Invariably, my only reward was catching a fleeting glimpse of the south end of a deer headed north.

Then, one day, the light bulb in my brain experienced an unusual burst of illumination which changed my deer-hunting strategy forever, and has since allowed me to successfully close the distance to countless numbers of bucks.

It all boils down to this logical conclusion: When deer are bedded during midday, they are virtually impossible to approach because a mature buck will have chosen a hiding location designed to provide the utmost security. To monitor his surroundings, he'll undoubtedly be on high ground, which enables him to have a good view of everything around him. Due to rising thermal air currents during midday, this high ground also allows him to use his nose to catch wafting tendrils of odors emanating from anything that may attempt to approach from below. Further, he's sure to be sequestered in dense cover, from which he'll have several escape route options because he instinctively knows that anything skulking around will have great difficulty penetrating such places without making forewarning noises.

Consequently, our hypothetical buck has four distinct advantages going for him during the midday hours. He's not moving but laying down, and is therefore difficult to see; and because of his carefully selected hiding location he can quite easily see, hear, or smell anything prowling around that may be a potential threat to his well-being.

Now insert a noisy, smelly, moving human into this picture and there is no question which creature has the upper hand!

During midday, deer are usually bedded, hidden from view and unapproachable. The best still-hunting success is at dawn or dusk when deer are on their feet, clearly visible, and preoccupied with feeding or other activities.

Now examine a comparable sneak-hunting scenario as it might unravel during the early morning hours of the day, and then again as evening dusk begins to settle in, and see how various components of the hunting equation dramatically turn around in your favor instead of the buck's.

Early and late in the day, our hypothetical buck is probably on his feet and moving around, which makes him far easier to see; not only is his body form better exposed to full view, but the motion receptors in your eyes will quickly draw your attention whenever he moves. Moreover, the reason he's on his feet is because he's doing something such as feeding, drinking, traveling to or from a food source or drinking site, rubbing a sapling with his antlers, tending a scrape, trailing a hot doe, or reaffirming his social ranking with other bucks. It's the very fact that he's engaged in some type of activity that makes him vulnerable because his senses and thought processes are at least partly preoccupied with the activity itself rather than what may be lurking (you) in nearby shadows.

LOOKING FOR DEER

Periods of light fog or drizzle, or gentle snowfall, seem to pacify deer and make for ideal conditions for sneaking up on a buck. Yet in the final analysis, a hunter's success hinges almost solely upon his eyes and how he uses them. In fact, I've often thought I'd be willing to trade my most expensive firearm for a far lesser gun and the vision of a hawk; it's been said that if a hawk could read, it could read a newspaper at 100 yards. Since a trade for such superior vision is obviously not possible, the only alternative a hunter has is learning to use the visual capabilities he does have to maximum effectiveness.

The problem with our human vision, as it relates to deer hunting, is that when we look off into the distance we tend to pinpoint our focus upon a small area, in an attempt to sort out details. As a result, if an animal 100 yards away is just ten yards outside your concentrated area of focus, you probably will not see it, especially if part of the animal's anatomy is concealed by cover. You may then conclude that no deer are around, begin your next forward advance, suddenly hear a loud snort, and only then see the deer for the first time as he bounds away.

All of this occurred because, contrary to the way we customarily view our surroundings, deer do not identify things by first looking at them in pinpoint focus. Instead, they scan their territory with a wide-angle perspective that allows them to catch the slightest movements, even when they are taking place around the outermost periphery of their visual scope. After that movement is detected, they narrow their focus on it for further classification.

Of course, successful sneak hunters know to move along at a snail's pace, with long pauses in between each step, so that the overall distance they travel during the day equals no more than 100 yards every half-hour. They've also trained themselves, when panning the terrain ahead, to not intently look at any particular feature, but to move their eyes slowly from right to left, then back again, concentrating upon picking up any movement that may be taking place in the distance. Only after no movement is spotted do they visually take the cover and terrain apart piece by piece. It's then, and only then, that they permit themselves to cautiously take another step or two forward.

Learn how to see deer by first panning the distance with wide-angle vision to detect movement. Then, pinpoint your focus to determine if it's a deer worth a still-hunting attempt.

TRACKING TIPS

When there is snow on the ground, many sneak hunters combine their still-hunting efforts with tracking in an attempt to double their chances of spotting deer. But it usually isn't worth it to follow tracks discovered in mid-afternoon. As emphasized in a previous section, deer customarily bed during midday, so the tracks probably were made earlier that morning and the animal may now be far away. But even if the deer should happen to be in the immediate area, remember how difficult it is to sneak up on a bedded buck that has all of his senses riveted upon his surroundings. This makes a good case in favor of following tracks only when they are discovered at dawn, because you can presume with a high level of certainty that the deer that made them is nearby, on his feet, and moving slowly.

One mistake committed by many hunters who have elected to follow tracks is to use the same exact route taken by the deer while continually looking at the imprints in the snow at their feet. What such hunters fail to realize is that when deer are traveling, they constantly monitor their back trails, which invites detection of a hunter's presence if he's on the same trail.

When tracking a deer, take a course parallel to the deer's so he doesn't look back and see you. Don't continually look at the tracks; focus your attention up ahead, hoping to spot the animal itself.

A savvy hunter, on the other hand, sneaks along a parallel course to the tracks, staying as far away from the tracks as he can while still being able to note the direction they are going; in most instances this distance will be thirty or forty yards to one side of the tracks or the other. Also, try to stay within thin cover, plotting each forward movement in such a manner that trees, brush, bushes, boulders, or other cover will help to hide your movements and make you less noticeable when a buck periodically looks back over his shoulder. Also spend a minimum of time looking at the tracks themselves, because the only thing they tell you is where an animal once stood. Where you want to train your attention is far ahead in the distance, where the tracks are leading, in hopes of eventually spotting the deer itself.

PUTTING ON THE STALK

When you finally come within sight of a deer, whether by following tracks or simply during the course of still-hunting, you may be able to successfully conclude the hunt then and there. Yet, just as often, you may spot the deer several hundred yards away. Or, as the animal continues to slowly move onward, it may inadvertently place some cover or terrain between the two of you. In either case, a renewed vantage point must be gained if there is to be any chance for a shot, and this means putting on a stalk.

When putting on the final stalk to get within shooting range, take it slow and easy, tread on soft ground to make no noise, and use intervening cover to conceal your approach.

First, try to second-guess the direction of the deer in the hopes of intercepting it at some point farther ahead. If it's possible to go around the backside of a steep knob, large rock formation, brushy thicket, or several acres of dense pines, and if such cover will hide any noise or movements you may make, it may pay to take off at a trot. Otherwise, since the animal is unaware of your presence, it's better to take it slow and easy.

It is imperative that the primary landscape features between the deer and the stalker not be disturbed or altered. In other words, the bobbing hat of a hunter moving along behind a hedgerow will alert the animal, as will other body movements such as your entire head and shoulders suddenly coming over the crest of a grassy knoll like a jack-in-the-box.

It's important to engage the stalk in such a manner that intervening terrain features may be utilized to block the view of the animal while advance movements are being executed. This means carefully (but quickly) selecting the route ahead, and using cover features such as logs, rocks, stumps, and the like that conceal most of the body most of the time, even if it makes the stalk longer in time or distance. Whenever you take a peek to reorient yourself to the animal's distance or perhaps its slightly changed travel direction, make sure your head is held low and to the side of the cover rather than high and above.

Should the animal be in sight and happen to look in your direction, freeze! Don't move again until the deer has given your general area the once-over and then returned to its previous activity.

What should you do if you make a mistake and snap a dry twig or step upon crunchy leaves that loudly broadcast your presence? The answer is to just accept it as part of the challenge of hunting deer, because it happens to the best of hunters. But also remember to immediately come to a halt for at least several minutes, not twitching as much as an eyelid.

If you step on a stick and it snaps loudly, freeze. A nearby deer will rivet his attention in your direction, but if there are no more sounds he'll forget what alerted him and go back to his former activity.

Lots of noises occur in the places where deer live, and they become accustomed to hearing everything from falling nuts, to squirrels rustling in ground leaves, to turkeys and grouse flushing from cover, to branches falling to the ground. In other words, deer are continually getting an earful.

However, deer also have the innate ability to catalog what they hear as either normal or potentially unsafe. As a result, if you commit some faux pas that alerts a deer, it will train its senses in your direction and wait for further noises to allow it to confirm what it initially heard. If you immediately come to a halt and make no more noises, the deer will eventually set its mind at ease and return to its former feeding or other activity. Therefore, it's not the occasional, blundering noise a hunter sometimes makes that spells his undoing, but the rhythmic cadence of continuing noises that to a deer signal danger.

Similarly, keep in mind that whitetails have relatively short attention spans. Biologists working with deer in large experimental enclosures say that three minutes is about the limit to their memory or any matter they may be engaging in before turning their attention to other thought processes. So when you make an occasional mistake—and you will—stop for several minutes, and any recognition that nearby deer may be giving that mistake will soon be forgotten.

One of the main difficulties in stalking deer is that decisions must usually be made quickly and accurately. But a hunter must be inventive, resourceful, and willing to put out just that little extra bit of effort that some others might not be so inclined to invest.

I remember one time when I took off my boots and walked in stocking feet across crunchy gravel to quiet my approach as I crossed a dry streambed. Another time I belly-crawled through 200 yards of thorns because the only suitable approach cover was close to the ground; as I field-dressed my buck, I looked and felt like a pin cushion. I can't remember how many times I've had to hold my rifle over my head while fording waist-deep streams.

ONCE-JUMPED DEER

Okay, you've been doing a commendable job of sneak hunting, and you finally spotted a nice buck, but then, while stalking to within acceptable shooting range, things went amiss. The deer momentarily glanced in your direction, apparently caught a slight flicker of movement on your part, and began loping away, white banner astern.

The correct strategy now is to simply sit down and be patient for at least fifteen minutes. Deer that are not outright spooked are often curious about what alerted them, and sometimes will circle around in hopes of identifying whatever it was made them nervous in the first place. This means that you may yet get a shot, especially if you pay close attention not to the direction in which the deer departed, but rather behind you and to either side.

If no deer returns to the immediate area after a full fifteen minutes, I suggest continuing to sneak hunt but making an elliptical loop to the right or left because the animal will certainly be keeping tabs on his back trail. Keep in mind that the deer probably didn't go far. Researchers studying animals wearing radio collars have determined that, unlike elk or mule deer, which may go five miles when spooked, whitetails invariably turn on their afterburners for only 200 yards or so, until they're just out of sight, whereupon they come to a halt, dive back into heavy cover, and resume their slinking behavior.

If you spook a deer and it dashes off, wait fifteen minutes to let him calm down. Then make a wide arc to get ahead of the deer's line of travel, and wait patiently. He may eventually close the distance and provide a shot.

Exactly how you pursue a "once-jumped" deer also depends upon the nature of the terrain. As a general rule, whitetails hold to the same type of cover and elevation as when you first moved them. Consequently, if you start a deer in a large stand of cedars, chances are the deer will stay in the cedars rather than breaking for nearby hardwoods. And if you start a deer in a swamp, it will probably remain in the swamp rather than evacuate for a nearby pine plantation.

Similarly, in mountainous terrain, a deer started on a side hill bench will predictably follow that bench on approximately the same contour level of elevation. Start a deer on a ridge and he'll probably continue to cling to that high ground for as long as possible. There are exceptions; if the deer comes to a saddle that allows him to slip unseen through a break in the ridgeline to the opposite side of the mountain, for example, count on him to take advantage of that natural escape hatch.

With knowledge of these behavioral traits in mind, you should be able to analyze the surrounding topography and make an educated guess as to where the animal might be farther ahead and, just as important, how to best approach it. Above all, don't rush. Think everything through because a once-jumped deer quite often presents himself for another shooting opportunity at a later time, but a twice-jumped deer is rarely so careless.

Finally, don't allow yourself to develop a fixation on one particular animal. You may be following tracks in the snow that suggest an impressive buck is somewhere up ahead, and you may have even jumped him once. But if you begin concentrating solely upon that one animal, to the exclusion of other deer that may be in the same immediate region, it may cost you. There may even be a bigger buck in the area, but you'll never see him if your focus is solely on the one you're following.

Chapter 17

Advanced Deer-Drive Maneuvers

I'd be willing to bet a week's grocery money that the traditional, worn-out deer-drive tactics you and your partners currently are using are largely ineffective.

In the least, the rather standardized deer drives so prevalent among today's whitetail hunters don't have much relevance when it comes to taking big bucks that have become programmed to react to drive situations in an entirely different manner than naive, younger deer. In short, today's big deer are panic-proof, and that means they're lot likely to get up and flee directly away from a conventional drive line.

THE GOOD OL' DAYS, WEREN'T

Unquestionably, driving deer a generation ago was quite a thing. Drivers carried not only firearms, but whistles, horns, and even discarded Halloween noisemakers upon occasion. The drivers dutifully stomped through the woodlands, hooting, hollering, and otherwise saturating the hills and hollows with a fusillade of approaching sounds. The din was supposed to move whitetails in the direction of stand hunters waiting as much as one or two miles ahead on logging roads, near clearings, or sometimes simply behind a tree near a suspected deer run.

Looking back, I wouldn't trade those memories, because they helped to shape my evolution as a deer hunter. But it is now evident that our drives—no matter how much fun and camaraderie we enjoyed—were confused, disorganized, and constituted little more than rudimentary gang hunting.

The drivers rarely had shooting opportunities, which is understandable because the noise they made enabled bucks to pinpoint their locations ahead of time and then sneak back through the spread-out drive line or circle widely and skirt the line altogether. Sometimes deer merely remained hidden in their beds in heavy cover until the drivers passed, and then bounded off in the opposite direction. Other times the commotion stampeded the deer, so that the animals did not follow predictable escape trails but squirted out in random directions. Consequently, even those standers who had been positioned on known deer trails seldom had shots, and those who did indeed see deer nearly always missed because the targets were in full flight.

None of this is to say that our mob-hunting efforts were dismal failures, because "even a blind hog will find an occasional acorn." But compared to the sophisticated drive tactics of today, those of the past were definitely inefficient, overly time consuming, and sometimes downright dangerous.

Further, there is no doubt in my mind that only a fraction of the bucks living in any given region were ever seen, much less shot at. Moreover, if someone even suggested that bowhunters could stage effective days, he would have been laughed out of town.

THE MINI-DRIVE CONCEPT

Small drive parties have a lot going for them. In these days of increasingly posted lands, a small group of courteous hunters stands a far greater chance of gaining access to private property than what happens when a caravan of vehicles pulls into the driveway of a predictably recalcitrant farmer to ask for drive-hunting permission. Even in the cases of state and federal lands, fewer hunters are easier to organize, position on stands, and keep track of on the drive line, which translates into greater efficiency.

Additionally, a gang of perhaps fifteen or twenty hunters can expect to make only several drives per day, simply because of the logistics involved in trucking so many hunters to their individual stand locations, lining up the drivers, and then at the appointed time beginning the long march cross-country.

Yet nowadays, with a smaller, hand-picked group of just a few hunters, we commonly stage up to twenty drives per day.

The first order of business is nominating one member of our hunting party to be the drivemaster. He doesn't have to be the best shot or have

Small drive parties are easier to organize than huge gangs of hunters. Silent drives are more effective than noisy drives because the animals move slowly, providing better shooting opportunities.

taken the most deer over the years; his main attribute should be that he's the individual who best knows the property to be driven and where the animals usually go. In this manner, with an aerial photo, he can show each member of the group what the terrain and cover to be driven looks like, where the drivers will begin, where each stand hunter should place himself, and what the animals are most likely to do. Be flexible about this, too. When the hunting party drives one particular area and then moves to a new drive location perhaps a mile or two away, it may be prudent to elect another drive-master who knows that particular property better than anyone else.

If no one in the group is intimately familiar with the terrain to be driven, hunting permission should be obtained well before opening day.

Always elect a drivemaster. He needn't be the most skilled hunter in the group, but should be the one who best knows the terrain and how the animals move when pushed by drivers.

This allows the group to do some pre-season scouting to learn the lay of the land, property boundaries, and anything else that will play a role in their hoped-for success. In fact, if it's private property, the best source of information is the landowner himself; he lives there year-round and probably sees deer almost daily.

Of course, whether it's private or public land, a key element in planning our drives is that we avoid huge, sweeping tracts of real estate. Such places take an eternity to drive but, more important, a small group of hunters simply cannot properly push the cover or guard all possible exits, and this allows the deer far too many escape options.

The terrain situations we particularly like to drive are very well defined. Invariably, each will consist of heavy cover bordered on at least two sides by open ground (such as prairie, pasture, or hay meadow) or some type of natural barrier such as a wide river-course or lakeshore, and seldom is the cover to be driven larger than twenty acres.

These self-imposed restrictions allow us to capitalize upon several different things. First, these little broken segments of private land or fragmented portions of state and federal lands are usually overlooked by other hunters. But we are perfectly happy to have these so-called leftovers, because they are the very places where cagey bucks like to hole-up as hunting pressure continues to mount on larger pieces of nearby real estate. Moreover, since whitetails are reluctant to expose themselves in open places, the well-defined perimeters of such swatches of cover allow us to better second-guess how the animals will move when pushed from their beds.

Examples of these mini-drive situations are almost too numerous to list, but among our favorites are the following: narrow gullies or ravines that are choked with downed timber but are no more than 200 yards in length;

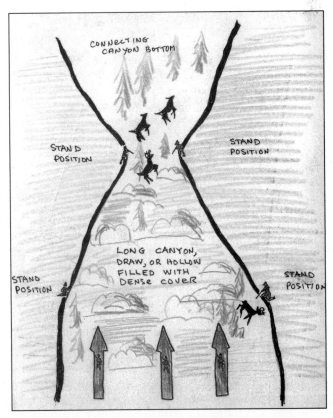

Driving small tracts of land is more effective because the deer have fewer escape options. An all-time favorite drive is through a bottomland where stand hunters can watch a constricted area the animals must squeeze through.

rectangular-shaped pine plantations no more than five acres in size, with immature trees that have dense whorls of branches close to the ground; rectangular-shaped cornfields no larger than five acres in size; willow bars along watercourses, in which the cover is no wider than fifty yards and no longer than 200 yards; narrow hollows with almost impenetrable stands of honeysuckle, laurel, or rhododendron; briar patches or jungles of laurel or multiflora rose that are no larger than ten acres in size; tag alder thickets bordering stream bottoms; swampy lowlands no larger than ten acres in size, and which have pole timber, blowdowns, at least several inches of standing water, and occasional dry hummocks; former fields and croplands now laying fallow and which have grown up in brush and thick regenerative saplings such as sassafras, sumac, poplar, and crabapple, no more than ten acres in size; and, finally, former burns and small clearcuts coming back into successive vegetation and thick young trees.

RAUCOUS DRIVES ARE OUT

We make use of silent drives. There is no hooting, hollering, and whistling. The reason for this is because we stage our drives during both bow and gun seasons. Especially when we're bowhunting, we don't want to risk wounding animals, as would be the case with deer wildly jackrabbiting through the cover. Much more to our liking is to just gently nudge the animals and hope they'll slowly sneak off in the direction of one of our standers.

For the most part, those hunters who are designated as drivers are actually engaging in still-hunting, although they move along a tad faster than what is recommended for a one-man still-hunting maneuver. The net result is that when deer are moved from their beds, they do not panic, which often rewards one of the drivers with a shot. Yet if the driver doesn't even see a particular deer move out ahead of him, his partner on stand farther ahead may have a chance at a slowly loping animal.

We also prefer to enact these mini drives on windy days. When the wind is gusting at more than eight miles per hour, a whitetail's sensory apparatus is greatly impaired. Under these conditions, a buck's ears cannot easily distinguish between the sounds of human footsteps and clacking tree limbs or rustling leaves. Moreover, a deer's eyes cannot easily detect a slowly moving hunter because of the competing movements of swaying stalks of vegetation. And although his nose may pick up the scent of one or more drivers in the distance, the erratic, swirling nature of the breezes will prevent the deer from pinpointing their exact locations or the routes they're taking.

As a result, the deer knows to lay down and hold tight. But if he is indeed moved from his bed, chances are better than even he'll travel only a short distance before quickly hunkering back down again.

Several years ago, we had an intriguing experience in Kentucky. There were three of us, and we decided to place Bob Murray on stand in a narrow corridor of high ground between two marshy bogs. Bill Jorgensen and I would then sneak hunt through an adjacent stand of cedars, hoping to push something to Bob. The wind was so fierce that I couldn't keep my hat on, so I folded it up and shoved it into my back pocket.

Moments later, a six-point buck got up just a few yards in front of me and, for brief seconds, just stood there, broadside. I loosed an arrow that flew harmlessly over his back. The deer took off, but ran only fifty yards before ducking back down again in waist-high grass. With my attention riveted on the deer's location, I began a careful stalk, eventually put the deer up a second time, and missed him again. The animal slowly ran just another fifty yards, but now was in the narrow corridor. A few seconds later I heard Bob Murray's victory yelp, indicating he had scored a good hit.

Under the windy conditions just described, staging mini drives is not unlike rabbit hunting. Of course, if there is no wind, you can still make drives, but the chances of the drivers having shooting opportunities are greatly reduced, especially if they are using archery tackle.

GAMES BIG BUCKS PLAY

In the past ten years, I'd venture a conservative estimate that I've participated in at least several hundred so-called mini drives. A number of specific happenings and events have so consistently repeated themselves that I now consider them almost axiomatic.

For one, when a mature buck is hiding in a relatively small piece of cover (less than twenty acres) and the cover is driven, that big buck will either be the first deer out of there or he won't come out at all.

Big bucks are extremely security conscious, and if they have reason to believe that their cover has been blown, they will not hesitate to leave the area, pronto! This insight is invaluable to an enterprising hunting party.

First, a hunter who is designated to wait on stand must exercise great care in hiking to his station. If a buck is bedded relatively close by and hears

If there's a big buck in the cover, he'll be the first to come out or he won't come out at all. If you suspect he's still in there, drive the cover again, but this time from a different direction.

the hunter moving into position, he will know that general area is a potential source of danger and he will not travel in the stand hunter's direction when he is routed out by approaching drivers.

So, when moving to your stand, take the long, roundabout way if necessary and sneak into position as quietly as possible. Also, once you've selected your vantage point, do not change your mind later and decide that perhaps somewhere else fifty yards to your right or left might be better. Your partners may have already begun the drive, and if the buck in question decides to leave the area by coming your way, he will be well ahead of any does or younger bucks in the region and therefore may very well detect your movement as you change locations.

If the drivers move one or more bucks through your general area but you are not presented with a shot, don't despair. Simply note the exact travel route used by the deer and file the information away in your memory bank. Then, when you drive the area again several days or weeks later,

Hunters placed in a tree stand should not move once they're in position. The drive may have already begun, and if the stand hunter moves, he's sure to be spotted by deer coming his way.

make the necessary adjustment in where you decide to wait on stand, for when the buck is moved yet again he'll likely use the same escape corridor as before.

By the same token, those hunters who are to act as drivers should allow their stand hunters plenty of time to get into position. It's simply a wasted effort to begin the drive five minutes too early, before the standers are well situated at their intercept locations.

If a combination of does and small bucks pass a stand hunter's location, the drive party can be certain any larger bucks in the immediate vicinity decided to hold tight; otherwise, they would have been the first ones out.

Actually, this is a far more common occurrence than most hunters realize. Big bucks select their hiding places with craft and cunning, and are reluctant to abandon these security havens because they know that rising from their beds and exposing themselves greatly increases their vulnerability. Consequently, when a hunter filters through their area, such deer quite often lower their chins right down onto the ground and then don't even blink.

Mature bucks are adept at sneaking around drive lines or remaining bedded until drivers pass and then getting up and slipping off in the opposite direction. Now is when the buttonhook drive pays off.

Therefore, after a drive has been concluded, if members of your group have reason to believe there still is a buck in the cover somewhere, there's only one thing to do: drive the cover a second or even a third time until the buck is either routed out or everyone becomes convinced he wasn't there in the first place.

Don't make the mistake of driving the cover in the same manner as before. Try something different, such as driving the cover in the opposite direction with your stand hunters placed in the vicinity of where the drivers began on the previous drive.

It's also worth mentioning that when you're staging drives on succeeding days, you should likewise avoid running your drives in the same manner as you did earlier. The only thing this will accomplish is educating the deer in that area.

Take a ten-acre, rectangular-shaped briar patch. This type of cover offers a buck a myriad of splendid hiding possibilities, but if your drivers consistently approach from the west, it won't take the buck in residence very long to learn where the danger is always going to come from.

The second time you drive the briars, have your drivers approach from the south, the next time from the east, and so on, assuming the nature of the terrain allows for such alterations. This way, especially if you are the lucky beneficiaries of windy weather, the deer will remain totally confused and not know which direction to expect danger. Nor will they ever know the surest escape route to avoid being detected by the hunters placed on stand.

WHEN DEER DOUBLE BACK

In many instances, a buck will hold tight in his bed, allowing a driver to pass, and then rise to his feet and attempt to slip out the back door, so to speak. He probably will not leave his chosen cover, but simply relocate his bed a slight distance away.

Imagine that you are in a jungle, trying to hide from someone. If that person passes close by, but you know you are well concealed, chances are you'll hunker down and stay put. Then, after that person passes and continues on for some distance, chances are you'll begin moving in the opposite direction in order to increase the distance separating you and your adversary.

White-tailed bucks behave much the same and there is one trick that will stack the odds in your favor. It's called by various names such as the buttonhook drive, or fishhook drive, but by any description the methodology is the same.

In using a rectangular-shaped pine plantation for purposes of illustration, let's place two hunters on stand along the far border of the pines. At the opposite end, two drivers space themselves a comfortable distance apart and begin sneak hunting through the pines toward their partners in the distance.

However, the two drivers don't actually proceed all the way through the pines to where their partners are on stand. They only travel perhaps two-thirds of the way through the pines, then they about-face and begin sneak hunting back toward their starting points. Quite often, one of the drivers will have an almost point-blank shot at a deer trying to slip away.

An intriguing aspect to all of this is that any buck that has doubled back to get behind the drivers may figure out what the drivers are up to when they engage in their buttonhook maneuver. Now the buck will double back yet a second time, to get behind the drivers once again. And this will take him in the direction of the hunters on stand!

THE ONE-MAN DRIVE

A solo drive is just the ticket when one member of a party has already taken his buck, while the rest of the hunters in the group want to wait on stands overlooking deer trails. The hunter who has already taken his buck can now help his partners fill their tags by playing dog.

Standers climb into their perches or ground blinds in pre-dawn darkness for the customary morning watch. But then, sometime in mid-morning, the lone driver begins hiking randomly through the cover without regard to wind direction. He makes no special effort to sneak or quiet his foot-falls. I often whistle softly to myself as though I'm a forestry worker doing a routine timber survey or a farmer counting livestock.

Since deer regularly see such people afield, a lone individual going about his business rarely alarms them. They simply get up and move out of his line of travel, using one of their established trails to relocate to an adjacent area. One driver moving in an erratic, snakelike pattern can keep deer slowly circulating all day, and eventually his partners watching vari-ous trails should have shooting opportunities.

Mini drives of the type described here can be quite challenging because they tax the ingenuity of all participants. But they're also loads of fun, and often result in new additions to the camp meatpole.

A one-man drive is effective when a hunter who has filled his tag wants to help his partners. If he slowly wanders around like a farmhand, with no attempt to be sneaky, deer will move out of his way and hopefully expose themselves to the hunters waiting on stand.

Chapter 18

Deer Decoy Tactics

Veteran bass anglers commonly say they'd rather experience the heart-stopping excitement of catching one largemouth on a surface plug than ten down deep.

It's equally true that once a deer hunter has watched a white-tailed buck charging a decoy he's set out near his stand, other types of hunting begin to lose a bit of their shine.

I suppose the reason for this is because today's generation of sportsmen want fast action, they want it now, and they want it to be extreme. And you

Using decoys is one of whitetail hunting's wrinkles. The action is not only exciting but wholly unpredictable.

just don't get that figurative kick in the pants by simply sitting in a stand for long hours hoping for a buck to eventually dawdle through your area.

Take the time in Georgia when I had an eight-pointer directly beneath my stand but couldn't shoot because the wild-eyed animal was repeatedly goring a fawn decoy I had placed near a bedded doe decoy. He'd throw the fawn into the air with his antlers, circle it with his head held low and neck hairs bristled, then gore it and throw it still again.

Eventually the lifeless, partly shredded foam decoy lay on its side and, now that the buck was finally convinced the fawn was dead, it rushed the bedded doe decoy and dug his antlers into her rump, trying to get her to stand so he could breed her. Obviously he didn't have much luck and moments later wandered off, never offering me a shot but leaving me with the feeling that my heart had almost imploded.

"Forget that a fawn has no spots during the fall/winter hunting season," Dave Berkley told me. "A buck doesn't reason that way. Like the males of most mammal species, his raw instincts tell him to first drive the offspring away from its mother, and kill it so that he can get on with uninterrupted breeding activities."

Berkley is the former president of the Feather-Flex Decoy Company, and when he heard of my experience with the fawn decoy he recalled an experience of his own.

"I'd tied the decoy to a strand of fencewire and then ran a fifty-foot length of clear monofilament fishing line to a nearby ground blind," Dave said. "By periodically jerking on the line, the decoy would jump and twitch as though caught in the fence. To add realism to the theatrics, I was using a screaming fawn call that mimics the bawls and bleats of a distressed or injured deer. What you'll attract is does, but if any of them are in estrus there's likely to be an amorous buck trailing close behind. Oh, one other thing. Be sure to take along some spare pacemaker batteries!"

Curiously, and this demonstrates the unpredictability of using decoys, I tried to duplicate Berkley's experience but wasn't successful in luring in either a doe or buck. This was on a Missouri hunt, and after just a few toots on my wailing fawn call, a coyote came loping in to investigate! Then a second dog arrived, and next thing I knew they were fighting and snarling—really going at it—over which one would get to kill and eat the bogus fawn. This caught me so off-guard that I made a slight movement at precisely the wrong time, and the wary coyotes took off.

As an aside, if you're interested in why a doe would respond to a screaming fawn call and fawn decoy, it's because does are highly maternal creatures. This causes them to instinctively rush to the defense of any offspring, even those which are not their own. If the rut is in progress and the doe is in estrus, a tending buck is sure to trail her right to your location.

All of this demonstrates that the use of decoys is so new that advanced, experimentally-minded hunters are encouraged to attempt ruses of their own, to learn what works and what doesn't.

THE EXCITEMENT CONTINUES

From my experience, using one or more decoys to attract a deer to your location can be lethal because, when a deer makes visual contact with what it perceives to be another deer, its motive for interacting with that deer is triggered by a desire for security, companionship, food, or sex.

Keep these tenets in mind when deciding when and where to use decoys, yet realize that the world of wild animals can switch from serene to chaotic in a millisecond. Take the time a smallish six-point buck responded to my buck tending-grunt, and came sneaking to within 100 yards of my stand. I had positioned a buck decoy at that range, and he hung up right there and would not come any closer. His ears told him another deer was on his turf, but he was confused because cover was partly obscuring the decoy from view. Where was the other buck he'd heard but could not see?

Just then, the decoy's tail swished back and forth, and the buck instantly rushed a dozen yards closer and craned his neck for a better look-see. Then he stamped a front hoof, trying to elicit further behavior from the counterfeit deer. I was sure that by now the buck could see the decoy's small rack, had pegged it as a subordinate, and knew he had nothing to fear.

Moments later the decoy's tail swished again, and with no further hesitation the six-pointer charged the decoy, drove the tips of his antler tines into its foam body, and knocked it over! Meanwhile, perched about fifteen feet above this ongoing spectacle, I drew and released an arrow and missed cleanly. At this, the buck wheeled and ran off thirty yards. Then he stopped and turned to look back.

Then, despite the fact that the decoy was now laying on the ground, its programmed timer, mounted within the hollow body cavity, caused the tail to flick again. Now the six-pointer, enraged to no end, charged and gored it once more. Then, in a moment of good fortune for me, the deer turned broadside and allowed me to slip an arrow through his ribs.

HOW DECOYS WORK

Other hunters who have joined the ranks of decoy users can undoubtedly describe similar incidents in what is rapidly becoming the most exciting method of bowhunting whitetails. I emphasize the word bowhunting because there is a consensus that using decoys during a firearm season when the woodlands are crowded can be dangerous. Also, check your state's regulations regarding the use of decoys; some states do not permit the use of decoys that can be mechanically activated with batteries or by remote-control lines.

In going back to a whitetail's gregarious nature, I've seen bucks and does rush into decoys and lick them, try to mate with them, and bed down among them. Yet because of their social orientation, it's necessary for them to establish a very well-defined pecking order within their ranks, and if this hierarchal ranking is violated, retribution of some sort is usually in the offing. In this regard, I've also seen bucks and does rush into decoys and kick them, bite them, horn them, or engage in a wide variety of bluffing and posturing.

Particularly during the rut, bucks interact aggressively with what they perceive to be rival bucks. This buck tries body-posturing in an attempt to intimidate another buck . . .

...and when that doesn't work, he charges and gores the decoy.

Mostly, however, whitetails are timid creatures that like to cling to the safety of dark shadows and dense cover, and are quite hesitant to expose themselves in open places. But this fear is cancelled when a deer sees others already standing in an open place, whereupon it then feels compelled to join the association.

I've experienced many instances, primarily when watching open feeding areas such as meadows, in which deer approached the open edge from deep cover and just stood watching, apparently trying to assure themselves it was safe to step out into the open and begin feeding. Yet when decoys are placed out in the open, deer commonly walk right out without hesitation. This is especially the case when a hunter is using decoys that are exhibiting a motion such as a flicking tail, which is the universal whitetail "all's well" signal.

THE RATTLING CONNECTION

It's important to mention that most decoys have removable antlers, so hunters can use the decoy as either a buck or doe. As a rule, the antlers are relatively small to simulate a subordinate buck that a larger dominant buck would not hesitate to approach and interact with.

Although buck and doe decoys can be used in a variety of ways, they are by far the most effective when used during the rutting season, in conjunction with antler rattling and grunting. But bear in mind that when a buck responds to the sound of antlers meshing in the distance, the animal expects to find one of two things. If he's the dominant buck in that neck of the woods, he expects to find two subordinate males jousting with each other and a nearby estrus doe in waiting. In this case, his mindset is usually to come in fast, make his hierarchal ranking known, drive the younger deer away, and then attempt to get cozy with the female.

If the responding buck is a subordinate animal, he doesn't quite know what to find at the scene of the rattling and grunting sounds he's heard. He may very well come upon two males that are even lower than he on the totem pole, or he may find two superior animals attempting to sort out their differences. Consequently, his mindset is to come in slowly and suspiciously, circling downwind and hanging back a safe distance until he has evaluated the situation.

This is why hunters who rattle antlers and grunt often report entirely different responses from approaching bucks.

Moreover, whitetails are very adept at pinpointing the exact location of rattling and grunting sounds. If they arrive at the scene and see no other deer, they immediately become suspicious and either remain back a cautious distance or altogether evaporate. Therefore, a decoy can provide the responding buck with the visual confirmation he needs to lure him in those final yards so the hunter can execute a close bow shot.

During a deer's final approach, refrain from rattling because the animal is sure to detect your movement. If you want to tease and coax him with a few additional grunts, be sure to use the type of short-stemmed grunt call that can be clenched between the teeth from the side of the mouth, thus allowing hands-free operation.

In fact, now's a good time to emphasize something else I've discovered. Whenever possible, use two or more decoys simultaneously. If you use only one decoy and it just stands there staring in one direction, approaching deer may become alarmed. If you use multiple decoys and can simulate them interacting, however, then the advantage will swing in your favor. One way to do this, if you have two doe decoys, is to position them in a grooming pose to create a far more natural scene. Ditto for an alert doe decoy standing next to a feeding doe decoy with her head down, or a buck decoy standing near a bedded doe decoy. Decoys made by Flambeau Manufacturing Company come in a wide variety of poses and are ideal for this kind of work; they are lightweight and hollow, and can be quickly dismantled, the head and legs stowed inside the body cavity for ease of carrying afield.

BUCKS AND DOES TOGETHER

In going back to the subject of deciding whether to use a buck or doe decoy, let the season and type of hunting you're engaging in dictate your choice.

For example, if my stand or blind is situated along the edge of an alfalfa meadow, and the rut is not in progress, I'm waiting for deer to come to a food source. Knowing in advance they might wait until it is almost dark before stepping out into the open, I'll place one or two doe decoys in the meadow.

I do this because whitetails live in a matriarchal society, and it is the adult does, not the bucks, who are the decision-makers. In a given band of deer, it is typically a mature doe that enters an open feeding area first, and by her presence tells others still hanging back in security cover that it's safe to venture forth.

Bedded doe decoys are effective because they have a relaxing effect on other nearby deer. They also simulate recently bred does attempting to conceive, which encourage bucks to investigate.

Doe decoys are also recommended during the peak of the rut, when amorous bucks are tirelessly checking their scrapes. If a buck is hanging downwind to scent-check a scrape, a doe decoy right next to the scrape, with its swishing tail, may communicate to the buck that "all's clear and safe, come and get me." A hunter can also try using a bedded doe decoy in an open clearing, because a bedded doe communicates through her body language that she has a calm and relaxed mindset. This, in turn, instills confidence in a buck that sees the decoy.

Does that have been bred recently commonly lay down in open areas because the bedding posture, with the female's body-weight exerting pressure upon the lower abdomen area, helps to facilitate conception. Yet since a doe does not always conceive during her initial mating sessions, this laying-down posture will draw the interest of nearby bucks that may be curious to see if the doe in question will allow additional breeding to take place.

In most cases, however, I prefer to use a buck decoy during the rut, simply because of the volatility that buck decoys can generate. I further like to have my set-up in the vicinity of scrape lines or scrape clusters (as opposed to single, isolated scrapes).

FINE-TUNING YOUR TECHNIQUE

While the best place to station a doe decoy is often in an open clearing bordering a forested region, the technique differs with buck decoys. We've already noted that a hunter will want to be in the immediate vicinity of scrapes. But, more specifically, the hunter will want to use what has become known as the "cribbing" approach to determining the decoy's placement. This means putting the decoy directly in front of some type of barrier or obstacle such as bushes, brush, or perhaps a fallen tree.

This "blocking cover" prevents any approaching buck from coming in from behind the decoy, and forces him to circle around in front and present you with a broadside or slightly quartering shot angle. In this manner, if your stand is placed about thirty-five yards from the decoy, you should have a twenty- or twenty-five-yard shot at a responding buck that walks between you and your decoy.

If putting cribbing behind a decoy is not convenient, another trick is to remove one of the decoy's antlers and substitute a broken antler in its place. A rival buck will always approach a decoy from its weak side, the side from which it cannot defend itself. So if the decoy is positioned with its weak side toward you, a responding buck should walk right between you and it.

In addition to decoys serving the purpose of bringing bucks into shooting range—by giving them a false sense of security so they'll step into open places, by sexually arousing them to the presence of a ready doe, or by challenging their hierarchal ranking—decoys have another important function.

A decoy occupies an approaching deer's attention and thereby diverts it away from the hunter's location, which is extremely important when bow-hunting animals at such close ranges that you can count their eyelashes. With the deer preoccupied with your decoy, he is far less likely to see you as you draw back your bow string for a shot.

In refining this technique, remember to never place a decoy directly facing your tree stand or ground blind, because a deer might turn to see what the decoy is looking at and see you in the process.

In the event that an incoming deer suddenly stops and begins stamping its front feet, or even snorting, don't worry. It's not your presence that is alarming him. He's simply trying to elicit some kind of response from the decoy. Eventually he will begin circling it in an attempt to look it directly in the eye. Relax and enjoy the show until he provides the shot you want.

Also consider using turkey decoys in conjunction with your deer decoys. Deer and turkeys get along very well in the wild, and are often seen feeding together along field edges and in forest clearings. I'll speculate the reason for this is that deer intuitively know that turkeys are very shy animals with super-keen senses that prevent predators (man or otherwise) from getting too close to them. Consequently, deer seem to feel safe, and behave in a relaxed manner when in the presence of turkeys.

Also, remember to never leave your decoys in place when you leave your stand. Take them with you or deer will eventually become suspicious of them.

Chapter 19

What Scientists Say About Deer Scents

With human beings, visual attraction is usually the stimulus that initiates a relationship with the opposite sex. Only later do other elements, often more mental than physical, enter the picture and either cement or destroy a relationship.

With deer, it's exactly the opposite. Since all does look alike, a buck is not attracted to one female over another based upon her physical attributes.

In the whitetail's world, the role of scents is solely for communication purposes, both when the animals have visual contact with each other and when they are not even in the immediate area.

Rather, he approaches, tilts his head back, inhales a few milliliters of her body odor, and allows the vomeronasal organ in the roof of the mouth to chemically analyze it. It is only then, through the gathering of this olfactory information that is he able to instinctively determine whether to pursue her and eventually bring the relationship to nature's logical conclusion.

Similarly, a doe can inhale a buck's scrape odor, chemically analyze it, and determine if he's a mature, healthy male that would be an acceptable mate.

WHAT DO WE REALLY KNOW?

According to deer biologist Dr. Karl Miller at the University of Georgia, the sense of smell is unquestionably the most important sense to whitetails. Although deer rely upon the detection of odors to warn them of the presence of predators and to help them find food, the most important function of scents is the role they play in communicating with other deer.

In addition to deer communicating their sexual readiness, a doe can recognize and identify her offspring as much as two years after they have been separated from her.

Further, a buck can determine through smell alone if other rival bucks are in the immediate area, as well as let them know of his presence. And both bucks and does can use the release of scents, and their sense of smell, to communicate danger, direction of travel, and dominance rank.

It should be emphasized that what we know or suspect about olfactory deer communication is based upon the use of sophisticated laboratory equipment in conjunction with actual observations of deer behavior. Moreover, all biologists agree that we don't know everything about the way deer glands function or their communicative purpose. Perhaps there are facets of whitetail body chemistry that we'll never have answers for.

Nevertheless, I believe that anyone who learns about a deer's known glands and the roles they play in the lives of deer will be more observant and mindful of the many unknowns that may be affecting our efforts afield, and this is sure to translate into a higher hunting success rate.

TARSAL GLAND SCENT

Bucks and does probably make greater use of their tarsal glands than any other, and they use them on a year-round basis. These appear as dark tufts of hair located on the inside of the rear legs at the hock, beneath which are enlarged sebaceous glands. The glands secrete a fatty substance that adheres to the hair.

Many hunters erroneously believe the tarsal glands have a rank odor, but the gland secretions themselves actually have no odor, or at least none that humans can detect. The musky odor is the result of the deer rub-urinating upon the glands and the chemical reaction the gland substance causes the urine to undergo.

All deer use tarsal scent to identify each other as to age, gender, and whether the deer in question is a non-resident intruder or a member of the local population. During the rutting season, bucks use tarsal-scented urine to communicate their level of social ranking to other bucks, while does use the scent to communicate their level of sexual readiness.

Releasing tarsal-scented urine is accomplished by the animal hunching up its spine, squeezing its rear legs together, then urinating so the flow runs down the inside of the legs, over the glands, and onto the ground. Although does and bucks randomly disperse tarsal scent throughout their

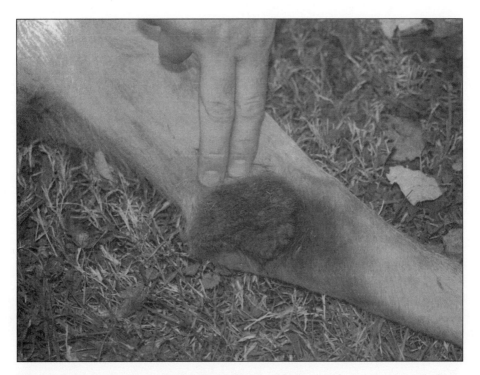

The tarsal glands release a musky-smelling odor that, like human fingerprints, is each deer's signature. It tells the animal's sex, age, and state of health.

home range, during the non-mating months it is most commonly deposited on trails and in the vicinity of bedding sites. During the mating season, both sexes commonly deposit the scent in and around buck-scrape areas (but not necessarily in the scrapes themselves).

One hunter intimately familiar with tarsal scent is Dr. Greg Bambenek of Duluth, Minnesota. Bambenek is the founder of the Osmic Research Company. He's a licensed MD who examines deer scents from a highly scientific viewpoint; his conclusions are based upon solid evidence, not any type of product hype.

"I agree with Karl Miller that in the sensory world of deer, hearing and vision are of secondary importance," Bambenek maintains. "Deer depend far more heavily upon their sense of smell. You see, hearing and vision require interpretive thought processes and mutual confirmation. But a deer's olfactory system is independent of conscious discrimination. It's a closed loop because, like a knee-jerk reflex, a scent signal leads to immediate reaction without forethought.

"Any quality brand of scent containing pure tarsal gland secretions is a hunter's best bet," Bambenek continues, "simply because it is effective on both bucks and does and on a year-around basis. Since tarsal scent uniquely identifies each individual deer, it's a type of scent that represents 'the new kid on the block' and will therefore literally pull deer to you to investigate. When shopping for scents, always keep in mind the oil of the tarsal gland, not urine, is the key to attracting deer.

"Conversely, my research has confirmed that urine-based tarsal gland scents, which sometimes are known as doe-in-heat scents or buck-in-rut scents, often have a reverse effect," Bambenek claims. "Ninety-five percent of the year, the scent of a doe in estrus doesn't make any sense to male deer and is more likely to alarm them. And a buck-in-rut scent is equally alarming to does, because when not in heat they don't want to be pestered by males."

Noted New Jersey naturalist Dr. Leonard Lee Rue III is in complete agreement. "Estrus-urine lures used before bucks begin making scrapes will probably spook them," Rue says. "And sex lures used three weeks before, or anytime after does begin reaching estrus will spook them. Such lures may attract a random buck that's trolling, but when does spook from the untimely scent and leave the area, the bucks go with them."

Also in agreement is Dr. James Kroll, professor emeritus at Stephen F. Austin University in Texas. He is charged with the responsibility of deer management programs on many large ranches.

"Tarsal glands from bucks are the only scent aids I've used with absolute positive results," the biologist says. Many hunters obtain tarsal glands not only from deer they've killed themselves but also from other hunters or at check stations or deer-processing plants. They then freeze them in plastic bags for future use, but this can be messy.

However, Dr. Kroll uses a novel technique. He soaks his glands in glycerine, which can be obtained at any pharmacy. Glycerine is a clear, syrupy liquid that absorbs the gland odor and, when later transferred to a small bottle, is a far more convenient way to use tarsal scent than carrying around the glands themselves.

Where should tarsal-gland scent be used? Most agree it can have positive effects almost anywhere that a hunter wants to attract the notice of resident bucks.

THE PREORBITAL GLAND ENIGMA

The preorbital gland is not a true gland at all. Located at the forward corner of the deer's eye, its function is not entirely clear. Although there is a visible glandlike slit, researcher Tom Townsend at Ohio State University says histological dissections of the area reveal no evidence of an underlying gland duct and therefore no secretion of scent. The occasional build-up of waxy material one sees in this area is apparently nothing more than the tear fluid residue that all mammals accumulate at their eye corners.

Biologist Karl Miller believes the preorbital slit, which is under voluntary muscular control, serves as a very close-range method of visual communication among deer. He has observed bucks flaring this "pocket" as a dominance display when facing off against each other. He says does also open this slit widely when closely tending their fawns, although the reason why is unknown.

This disputes the wives' tale often circulated by novice hunters that after a buck makes a scrape and mutilates the tree branch hanging over it, he deposits scent upon the branch from his so-called preorbital "glands." Biologists say the deer is actually depositing scent upon the branch from the nearby forehead glands.

FOREHEAD GLAND SCENT

Forehead gland scent apparently comes into play only during the rutting season. And even though bucks and does both possess forehead glands, only the most mature dominant bucks have highly active forehead glands, says Georgia biologist Larry Marchington.

These glands are actually very tiny sweat glands that carry each deer's hormonal code. Numbering in the hundreds, these glands cover the entire forehead area between the eyes and the bases of the antlers. The buck uses them to deposit scent to communicate with other deer.

Just beneath a deer's scalp are hundreds of tiny sweat glands that carry each deer's hormonal code. Bucks deposit this scent on antler-rubbed trees and licking branches over scrapes. In does, it is not known what role the forehead glands play.

Research findings by Georgia's Dr. Tom Atkeson suggest that forehead gland scent deposited upon antler rubs and tree branches hanging over scrapes serves three purposes. Since mature, dominant bucks are the first to rub saplings in the early fall, scent deposited upon such rubs tends to chemically inhibit or repress the testosterone and libido levels of younger, immature males. Simultaneously, these chemical residues on rubbed saplings serve as "priming pheromones" that, when licked by does, accelerate the onset of their estrus cycles, bringing them into heat earlier than if a dominant buck was not in the area soliciting companionship. And when forehead gland scent is deposited upon a tree branch hanging over a scrape, it is a warning to other bucks passing through the area to stay away from that proclaimed breeding area.

There are several ways hunters can use these insights to good advantage. For one, get out in the early fall and try to find the very first antler rubs, because they are the work of the dominant bucks in the region. Younger, immature bucks don't begin rubbing trees until as much as three weeks later.

I've often found myself sitting in a stand near a trail where numerous trees have been rubbed, and automatically knew when to pass up shots at bucks traveling by. If a deer walking down a trail displays a timid personality in the vicinity of a rub, you may wish to decline any shot that presents itself. This submissive body language, usually in the form of the head held low and a sway-backed posture with the tail clamped against the back of the legs, is a clear sign the buck is an immature subordinate and that a larger buck actually made the rubs before you.

Additionally, if a buck comes to a scrape you're watching and appears more interested in inspecting the broken overhead branch than checking the scrape itself, you can be sure of one thing: that particular buck ranks low on the dominance scale, and it was not the animal that made the scrape.

INTERDIGITAL GLAND SCENT

Bucks and does possess interdigital glands on all four feet. The glands are located between the toes, and secrete a yellow, waxy substance that has a rancid odor which is deposited in very minute quantities every time the deer takes a step.

According to Dr. Miller, who has chemically analyzed the gland secretions, they're comprised of fatty acids of different volatilities, which means their odor molecules evaporate at different rates.

As a result, the odor of a deer's tracks changes over time, leading biologists to believe that interdigital gland secretions are used by males and females year-round as a means of communicating their direction of travel. For example, fawns and yearlings that lose sight of their mothers can sniff her tracks and determine in which direction the odor is most intense; this enables them to follow in that direction to catch up. In the spring and summer, separated bachelor bucks can do the same to regroup. And during the rut, bucks can trail does to eventually locate them and determine their state of estrus.

Unfortunately for the deer, other mammals also possess this ability. That's why it's common to see predators such as free-ranging dogs or coyotes come upon a deer trail and correctly turn right or left to follow the deer's tracks in the direction the animal was traveling.

One way a hunter can use this insight involves observing deer behavior to determine the frequency with which various trails are used. If a slowly-walking buck or doe repeatedly puts its nose to the ground but is not eating, it is smelling interdigital scent, indicating other deer frequently are using that trail.

METATARSAL GLANDS SOUND THE ALARM!

The whitetail's metatarsal glands are also shrouded in mystery. While the tarsal glands are located on the inside of the hind legs and have hair tufts that are darkly stained during the rut from urine repeatedly passing over them, the metatarsal glands are located on the outside of the deer's hind legs and are surrounded by white tufts of hair.

Research conducted at UCLA, with mule deer and black-tailed deer, revealed that the animals use their metatarsal scent to warn other nearby deer of impending danger. In one study, metatarsal scent was extracted from a penned mule deer and placed in the watering tank at another deer pen. For several days, the animals there would not approach the tank to drink until it was eventually emptied, thoroughly cleaned, and refilled with fresh water.

"In the world of whitetails, there's strong evidence that metatarsal scent also is an alarm pheromone," Bambenek says. "This is the scent they release when they're being chased by dogs or coyotes, when they panic if they feel they've been cornered, or when their bedding sites are disturbed.

"Be sure to smell every scent you buy," Bambenek advises. "If you ever find one that has a faint garlicky odor, the company in question didn't do any research and included metatarsal gland secretions. Don't throw the scent away, however, because it can be used as a very effective trail block to divert deer traffic in a different direction."

NEW RESEARCH

The latest glands to be discovered were entirely unknown just a few years ago. One group, called the preputial glands, are clusters of greatly enlarged sebaceous glands within the buck's penile sheath, and have very long hairs that extend from the sheath. Several biologists have speculated the preputial glands play a role in mating behavior, perhaps helping bucks achieve their characteristic rutting odor and thus facilitating the break-up of bachelor groups that predominate throughout the spring and summer.

Another group of glands are within the deer's nasal passages, but this is such a recent finding that we don't have any conclusive answers as to their function. It has long been observed that when bucks are in the presence of branches hanging over scrapes, they lick them, chew upon them, rub them across their nose and tongue, and deposit all manner of saliva, slobber, and drool. They're undoubtedly conveying some type of information to the next deer that passes through the immediate area and inspects the branch.

With regard to any of the glands and the scents they secrete, it's important for hunters to keep in mind that deer communicate olfactory information in a very short-range context.

Biologists claim that beyond 250 yards, which constitutes a whitetail's so-called "security zone," deer are not likely to react to any odor carried by the wind. "React" is the key word here. By the time the odor has carried that distance, its molecular structure has become so diluted that it is not capable of triggering the animal's olfactory chemoreceptors, which must be stimulated in order for a behavior response to follow.

So when using commercial scents in conjunction with a knowledge of how deer themselves use such gland secretions, don't make the mistake of thinking that deer will funnel in your direction from all parts of the county. In fact, with regard to tarsal scent, some researchers have concluded that a deer's recognition distance is limited to less than twenty-five yards.

WHAT ABOUT COVER SCENTS?

You've seen them in sporting-goods stores and mail-order catalogs, dozens of scent brands in a multitude of aromas touted to mask human odor. Some of the more popular ones (with hunters) are apple scent, pine scent, skunk scent, and fox urine.

Yet the overriding factor in using any type or brand of cover scent is really quite simple: always use a cover scent in its proper context.

When using a cover scent, make sure it is indigenous to the area you're hunting. Using fox urine in a region where there are no foxes, or pine scent in an area where there are no conifers, only serves to advertise your presence, not hide it.

For example, if you're hunting in or around an apple orchard, any brand of apple scent may do a fine job of disguising your human odor. However, if you're hunting in a region where the only apples are those found in a grocery store, the deer in that region haven't become familiar with the smell of apples. Therefore, if a buck catches a whiff of your apple cover scent, the smell will be alien to him. It will be strange, out of place. And anything that a deer suddenly detects in its environment that is abnormal and doesn't belong there is sure to trigger an alarm reaction and probably cause him to vacate the area.

"Most hunters also fail to consider that since a deer's sense of smell is ten thousand times more acute than that of humans, the animals are able to distinguish very subtle differences in what we might consider to be the same odor," Tennessee biologist Darren McVey explains. "In other words, several different 'pine' cover scents produced by different companies may all smell the same to us. But if one of those products is derived from the oil of white pine, that particular scent may spook deer when used in a region where the predominant conifer species are balsam fir, hemlock, cedar, or jackpine. Moreover, many cover scents don't contain natural ingredients but are synthetic (chemical) blends. So always be sure to read the bottle's label to see if it specifies the type of vegetation the scent simulates."

"The same is true with animal-based cover scents such as fox or coyote urine," Bambenek points out. "If foxes or coyotes are not native to the specific place you hunt, using such cover scents only serves to advertise your presence, not hide it."

Since the matter of using commercial cover scents is so unpredictable (and unscientific), many hunters use only natural scents indigenous to their hunting areas. For example, my friend Tom Parker hunts a long, brushy bottomland on a dairy farm in southern Ohio. He uses just one type of natural scent to blend with that particular environment. When hiking to his stand, he steps in a cow pie and smears some of the dung on the soles of his boots. Not only does the odor of Guernseys waft about his stand to naturally camouflage his human odor, but he also gets the benefit of leaving cow scent on the trail he uses to access his stand—and that is exactly what deer expect to smell there. In addition to stepping in livestock dung, or deer pellets, you can also step in mud or swamp muck if you happen to be in riverbottom terrain or a marshy lowland.

Another trick is to take a small spruce or pine bough and crush the needles in your hands to release their aromatic oils, then rub your hands on your trousers and jacket sleeves. Equally effective is trimming a few small branchlets from a conifer and placing them in the bag where you stow your hunting garments, so the natural odor will permeate the fabric.

If you're hunting in the vicinity of an orchard, slice an apple or other fruit and rub the exposed, juicy halves onto your pantlegs and jacket sleeves. You can do the same with other strong-smelling farm foods being grown locally, such as onions or cabbage.

There are other examples as well, but the idea is to smell like you belong wherever you happen to be, rather than standing out as different. It is always the out-of-place odors, or those used at the wrong time of the year, that are most readily detected by deer and cause them to become suspicious.

SQUEAKY CLEAN

For any type of scent to be effective, a hunter cannot allow it to be over-powered by the odoriferous grunge and grime the human body produces every day.

Most hunters recognize the value of bathing with a non-perfumed soap before hunting. But do you know the brand names of legitimate odor-free soaps? Some found in grocery stores may have labels that state they're perfume-free, but if they contain cold cream, cocoa butter, lanolin, or other similar ingredients, they may leave odor residues on your skin that are readily detectable by deer.

The most popular, and effective, odor-free soap is Phisoderm, available at any pharmacy. Technically, this is not really a soap. It's a body cleanser, and it's widely used in hospitals by doctors when they scrub before surgery; it's also used in bathing post-surgical patients to minimize skin bacteria and thus infection. And skin bacteria, as we know, are precursors of body odor.

But with any body cleanser or perfume-free soap, the key to using them is to bathe immediately before leaving home or camp for the day's hunt, not the night before. The body's natural production of skin bacteria is an ongoing process, and the longer the bacteria remains on the skin and exposed to the air, which allows it to grow and multiply, the more body odor you produce.

Consequently, if you were to shower at 10:00 p.m., just before going to bed, by the time you found yourself sitting on stand the following morning, your body would have had a full eight hours to farm a tremendous crop of skin bacteria. It might not be so acrid and pungent to cause your hunting partner's eyes to water, but it will nevertheless be noticed by downwind deer.

IT'S A WASH!

Of course, a clean body is of little advantage if your hunting garments reek of household odors, pet odors, tobacco, or the week-old salami sandwich you forgot about in your coat pocket.

Garments are highly porous because they are made of natural or synthetic fibers woven together; the millions of tiny air pockets between the fabric threads trap air molecules and give the material its insulating quality. Yet, because odor is also a combination of various types of air molecules, these become trapped as well.

There has been a lot written about washing your clothes in a non-scented soap, but one that has become especially popular with deer hunters is Sport-Wash (mentioned in Chapter 12). This soap leaves clothes entirely odor-free.

Sport-Wash is designed not only for cotton and various synthetics, but also is well-suited to the home laundering of other fabrics such as wool and garments insulated with down, Thinsulate, GoreTex, and others. In the past, hunters had to take these garments to a dry cleaner, at considerable expense, and got them back reeking of dry-cleaning solvent. No more.

After washing, hang your hunting clothes outside to air-dry in fresh breezes. If this isn't possible and you must use your home dryer, be sure not to use a perfumed fabric softener. By the same token, do the same with your bath towels. It's self-defeating to wash your clothes with a perfume-free detergent, then bathe with a perfume-free body cleanser, then dry yourself with a towel saturated with lilac or some other fragrance.

If your garments and towels must be stored inside your living quarters, or transported to your hunting destination before being put on, store them in plastic bags.

It's also worth saying that most serious hunters are almost fanatical about their pre-hunt routines. They don't wear their boots and outer garments during the drive to their intended hunting locations, they don't stop along the way to pump gas or eat breakfast in a diner where the air is grease-laden and filled with smoke, and at their parking area they don't stand around idling vehicles spewing exhaust fumes.

Why permit a wide range of odors associated with human activities to hitchhike to your stand?

Instead, they gas up the night before, bring a thermos bottle and snack to eat on the road, and then take their outer hunting wear from plastic bags and finish dressing just moments before hiking to their stands.

To illustrate the dedication many hunters have to this effort, my hunting pal Tom Tompson once had the misfortune of getting a flat tire on the drive to his morning stand location.

"By the time I got the tire changed," he lamented, "I smelled like I had just finished working a shift at a rubber-vulcanizing plant. I didn't want to risk spooking the buck I had so carefully patterned near my stand area, so I canceled that morning's hunt."

Upon arriving back home, Tompson began de-programming himself by washing and drying his clothing and then bathing again. By the time he finished, it was early afternoon, so he immediately left home and drove to his hunting location for the evening watch. He didn't see his buck that day, but he did see it—and take it—the following morning.

In camp or at home, wash your clothes in a scent-free detergent and then hang them outside to air-dry. If you then must travel by vehicle to your intended hunting area, stow your boots and outer garments in plastic bags.

Chapter 20

Be An Expert Venison Chef

Deer hunters and their families have long maintained a love-hate relationship with venison. There's no clearer evidence of this than what happens when the hunt is over and individuals prepare to depart camp for home. Some of those hunters will guard their venison as if it's gold. Yet others, after sawing off their buck's antlers, will eagerly donate their deer meat to anyone who will take it.

Those who dislike venison are almost always the products of previous experiences, in which an inept hunter—often themselves—mishandled the meat at some point between field-dressing to kitchen.

Conversely, those who give venison high ratings have invariably had the good fortune of being taught how to properly care for the meat from the time the animal expired to the eventful moment when a platter of the succulent steaks or chops arrives at the dinner table.

The crux of the problem is that the various cuts of venison look very much like beef. As a result, novice chefs commit the error of first trying to cook it like beef, and then subconsciously expecting it to taste like beef.

In trying to cook their venison as they would beef, they usually ruin it. And when they taste it and it doesn't have the beef-like flavor and texture they have been anticipating, an alarm bell rings.

Next, they predictably turn up their noses and begin claiming the meat is spoiled or has such a wild and gamy flavor that it's just not to their liking. What has actually happened is that they've become innocent victims of their own sensory deception.

CHARACTERISTICS OF VENISON

Aside from the fact that deer and cows eat a wide variety of foods, which influence their flavors, deer are involved in much higher levels of exercise than cows. This means there is a significant difference in the fat content of the two animals, which in turn governs the textures of the meat.

Beef, by content, possesses twenty-five percent fat, while venison possesses only four percent fat, which makes venison such a nutritious choice among health-conscious individuals who want to reduce their fat and cholesterol intake; incidentally, venison has less cholesterol than chicken. Also, a high percentage of the fat found in beef is woven interstitially throughout the tissue fibers, while nearly all of the small amount of tallow possessed by deer is layered across the front shoulders, down the back, and across the rump, and should be removed during butchering because it does not freeze well.

As a result of how deer and cows "carry" their fat, the tissue structure of beef is relatively fine-grained and highly marbled, while venison is more coarsely grained and possesses virtually no marbling.

Because beef has a high fat content, it can withstand a longer cooking time than an equal quantity of venison and still remain tender. But since venison already is a lean, dry meat to begin with, using the same length of cooking time as you would for beef will make it as tough as boot leather; this is because there is little marbling fat to internally baste and lubricate the tissue fibers as they cook, as is the case with beef.

COOKING TIPS

One secret to tender venison is not a particular recipe you may elect to use but the length of cooking time the meat is subjected to. Prime cuts such as the backstrap steaks or chops, or the sirloin-tip steaks or round steaks from the hindquarters, are most often cooked by a dry-heat method such as pan-frying, using the broiler in your oven, or grilling the meat over coals. Yet none of these cuts should ever be cooked beyond the point of medium-rare, as this stage is when they are the most tender, succulent, and juicy. Forget that you may prefer your beef steaks cooked medium, medium-well, or even well-done. As we've emphasized, venison is not beef.

Similarly, while larger cuts of venison such as sirloin-tip roasts, rump roasts, and rolled shoulder roasts are usually baked in an oven, they should likewise never be overcooked.

A meat thermometer is essential in monitoring the cooking progress of a roast or other large cut of venison. Insert the thermometer so the bulb is in the center of the thickest part of the meat, and ensure that the bulb does not touch the bone or bottom of the roasting pan.

Bake the roast only until it is medium-rare and possesses a blush of bright pink in the middle. If you look at your meat thermometer, you'll see a graduated scale paired to the desired doneness of various types of meat such as beef, pork, and fowl. Since venison won't be listed on the scale, you'll have to go by temperature alone, but this is no problem. To achieve a roast that is medium-rare, allow it to cook until its internal temperature registers 145 degrees.

RECIPES

Every serious deer hunter should have several game cookbooks. There are many on the market containing hundreds of fail-safe ways to prepare venison. Following are just a few of my own favorites.

Venison Meatloaf

1½ pounds deer burger
1 cup cracker crumbs
2 eggs, beaten
1 8-ounce can tomato sauce
½ cup chopped onion
2 tbs chopped green pepper
1½ tsp salt
1 medium bay leaf
dash thyme
dash marjoram

Make the deer burger by grinding together 1 part beef suet to 3 parts venison. In a bowl, combine all ingredients and knead together well with your hands. Dump mixture into a bread pan and tap on a hard surface several times to settle the contents. Bake at 350 degrees for 1 hour. Serves 4.

Venison Goulash

1 12-oz package wide noodles
1 pound deer burger
1 onion, chopped
2 stalks celery, chopped
⅓ cup ketchup
1 4-oz can sliced mushrooms
1 14-oz can tomatoes, undrained
2 tsp salt
½ tsp black pepper

Cook the noodles according to package instructions. Meanwhile, brown the deer burger in a skillet. Drain off the grease, then add the onions and continue cooking until they are clear. Stir in the cooked, drained noodles, ketchup, celery, mushrooms, tomatoes, salt, and pepper. Cover the skillet and simmer on very low heat for ½ hour. Serves 4.

High-Country Buttermilk Steaks

2 pounds backstrap steak meat or sirloin-tip meat
cooking oil
1 cup buttermilk
flour

Cut the steak into thick cubes, then pound each with a meat mallet until no more than ½ inch thick. Place the meat in a bowl and cover with the buttermilk. Allow the steak to soak for 2 hours, turning occasionally, then dredge the pieces with flour and panfry. Serves 4.

Venison Italiano

2 pounds backstrap steaks or sirloin-tip steaks
½ cup olive oil
½ tsp garlic powder
½ tsp Worcestershire sauce

Thoroughly blend the Worcestershire sauce, olive oil, and garlic powder in a bowl. Then use the mixture to baste the steaks as you broil them in your oven or grill over charcoal. Serves 4.

Iron Range Venison Roast

1 3-pound rump roast
1 tsp fennel seed
1 tsp sage
1 tsp sugar
1 tsp salt
½ tsp black pepper

Take a rolled rump roast and remove the string ties so you can open the meat. Spread the venison out as much as possible and make numerous scoring cuts across the meat with a knife. In a bowl, blend all of the seasonings, then sprinkle over the meat. Roll the meat back into its original shape and make new string ties. Insert a meat thermometer, drape the roast with bacon strips, and set in a shallow roasting pan. Roast at 325 degrees until the internal temperature registers 145 degrees. Serves 6.

Foiled Again Pot Roast

1 2-pound rump roast or rolled shoulder roast
1 envelope dry onion soup mix
1 cup water

Place the roast in the center of a square sheet of heavy duty aluminum foil and bring the edges up around the sides to form a pouch. Pour the water over the roast, then sprinkle on the onion soup mix. Now pinch together the edges of the foil to form a tight seal to trap steam, and place the pouch in a shallow roasting pan. Place in a 325-degree oven for 1½ hours. If desired, thicken the gravy with a bit of flour. Serves 4.

Crockpot Roast

1 2-pound rump roast or rolled shoulder roast
1 can condensed mushroom soup
salt and pepper

Place the roast in a crockpot, salt and pepper, then pour the condensed mushroom soup over the top. Cover and slow-cook on low heat for 4 to 8 hours. Serves 4. If there are leftovers, the following day shred the meat, heat along with the remaining gravy, and serve for lunch on thick slices of Texas toast with chives sprinkled on top.